OCR

D0934470

THE Secret
TO MAKING YOUR
Invention
A REALITY

By David A. Fussell
Proverbs 19:8 L.B.

A workbook from the popular tape series "The Secret
To Making Your Invention A Reality." Includes a selection
of the most important inventor forms and suggested contracts
needed by the inventor. The author encourages the user of the
workbook to contact a registered patent attorney prior to
using any suggested contract contained herein.

Order this book and the tape series from:
VENTUR-TRAINING L.P.
3794 Meeting Street
Duluth, GA 30136
1-800-334-0233

First Edition

Library of Congress Catalog Number: 94-78998

ISBN: 0-9639336-1-2

Tape Series and Workbook Produced
By Jonathan Bulkley, J.B. Audio

Workbook Edited By
Cynthia F. Stephens

Printed in Atlanta, GA

Tape series and workbook written by

David A. Fussell, founder and president of

VenturSource International Consulting, Inc.

and Ventur-Training, L.P.

Table of Contents

Introduction

This workbook is a companion to the four-tape cassette album, **The Secret To Making Your Invention A Reality**. Both are produced by Ventur-Training, L.P. and David A. Fussell, its founder and president.

David A. Fussell is a prolific inventor, product designer and lecturer. He has written and published a number of articles for invention trade publications. He is an expert on inventing and product development. In addition to developing his own products and successfully licensing many of these, he works with companies and individual inventors to assist them in developing and introducing their products to market.

Mr. Fussell's goal in providing you with this material is for you to learn his successful methods of new product development. He feels confident that once you have listened to and comprehended the information offered in this tape series and workbook, you will possess the secrets necessary to maximize your earning potential in your invention and licensing venture.

The following information is intended to cover product development in general. Although a great many of the products that are invented fall within the "general" category, there are exceptions. When necessary, you should seek additional professional assistance and advice concerning your particular product.

This workbook includes some fill-in-the-blank passages and end of chapter questions to help you cement your learning process and document your plan of action. You are encouraged to thoughtfully respond to these facilitators in order to gain the greatest benefit from this material.

Foreword

"I've got a great idea! Now what do I do?"

Over the years, I have heard that question thousands of times. The joy of a new idea and the pride in solving a vexing problem evolve quickly into the dilemma of what to do next.

America leads the world in new product development and technological breakthroughs, and the 1990s may well be the Decade of the Inventor. Our society and the way Americans work are changing. Huge corporations are "downsizing" forcing many to reevaluate their career options. Fax machines, user friendly computer software programs, modems and sophisticated telephone services combine to make a small business more viable than ever. "Be your own boss." captivates the American spirit today much as "Go west, young man!" sparked the imagination of an earlier generation.

As society's work habits change, the inventor/entrepreneur is achieving a newfound respect. As major corporations downsize, the positive economic impact made by small businesses and new product developers is dramatically apparent. These forces have combined to provide a dynamic atmosphere supportive of creativity and new ventures.

Getting that "great idea" is like striking gold, but developing it into a product is as long and demanding a process as any successful gold mining venture has ever been! One of the greatest challenges facing the inventor is the one he or she recognizes immediately: "What do I do next?" This question is quickly followed by, "Who can I trust?" Luckily for today's inventors, the answers are more readily available than ever. Government sponsored programs and facilities, university entrepreneur centers, and local and national inventor organizations offer a wealth of support and guidance to the novice inventor.

As with any new venture, the person with that "great idea" should seek the advice and counsel of those who have gone before. Successful inventors who have learned the hard way, making mistakes and tasting success, are the best source of down to earth answers. David Fussell has known the joys, frustrations, failures and successes... and he learned to combine these experiences in a positive way and has produced a map for other inventors to follow.

Mr. Fussell presents the total picture of what it takes to move from "great idea" to successful product. Each step is outlined in detail with the understanding that the novice inventor is holding down a job, involved with family responsibilities and operating on a budget. He also understand that the great majority of inventors are not interested in starting a manufacturing facility to produce their products. Mr. Fussell developed a unique method of product licensing, and he shares the concept and method with the reader.

David Fussell's tape series and workbook answer the question, "What do I do next?" for any inventor at any stage of development. The novice receives an education in new product development and the pro will glean inside tips never before considered. Those who dare follow their dream and turn their "great idea" into a profitable reality will benefit immeasurably from David Fussell's advice and practical, down to earth counsel.

Creativity, invention and innovation are the hallmark of the 1990s and the pages that follow are every inventor's guide in their exciting quest to be part of the Decade of the Inventor.

Colorado Springs, CO   Joanne M. Hayes

August 21, 1994   Publisher, INVENTORS' DIGEST

America's heritage is rich with inventors - both men and women who dared to be different; who were willing to reach out into the unknown; who had a burning passion - a dream that somehow they could not shake from their minds. These few creators mentally processed information in a different manner than those around them.

You see, most people dismiss as fantasy or ridiculous those moments of genius that skip across our conscious and subconscious minds. But a select few are able to recognize and capture those unique impressions, hold on to them, live with them and develop them. Even when faced with the ridicule of our peers, we never entertain the thought of the remote possibility that the concept we have nurtured might not work. These are the creators, the inventors, the entrepreneurs, the movers and shakers who built America, and to whom the future belongs. This is not just my story, but the story of inventors who came before you and me and those who will follow.

There are always those who doubt. If you are in any way different from others, you can expect to be laughed at. It's been said that "If you rise above the crowd, you are likely to get a tomato in your face!" Those who laugh at your inventiveness, deny themselves a part of their birthright as Americans; a birthright of creative opportunity, and the freedom to follow one's dreams; the freedom to create and to build a better life for themselves and their neighbors.

If you are an experienced inventor, I trust this material will help you discover a small pearl of knowledge; something new that you had not thought of that will increase your chances of financial success. If you are just beginning your journey into the unique world of inventing and developing new products, you have taken an important first step by purchasing this material.

I am grateful that God has granted me the wisdom to create and develop new products. I'm also grateful for the opportunity to pass on the knowledge with which I have been entrusted. When you begin a new endeavor you are limited only by your lack of knowledge or your inability or lack of initiative to seek out and obtain that knowledge.

> *One of the most powerful things in our universe is <u>knowledge</u>.*

The journey you are about to embark on is long and difficult, and may be full of disappointments and set backs. Inventing is not easy work. Thomas Edison said, "Invention is two percent inspiration and ninety-eight percent perspiration." For all of us there are also those moments of doubt and fear of the unknown. T.S. Elliot put it this way, "Between the idea and the reality, falls the shadow." But the important thing for you to realize is this - it is now your turn at bat! You will never hit a home run if you never commit to swing at the pitch.

However, there are risks in this type of venture. So let me warn you that over 300,000 people in the United States lose money each year trying to market new products.

> *I've designed these materials to help you avoid the most common pitfalls faced by inventors. If you implement and follow the course of action outlined in this text, you will greatly increase your chances for successful product development and market introduction. In addition I'll share with you some secrets that have helped me successfully develop new products.*

OVERVIEW OF THE DEVELOPMENT PROCESS

I am often asked, "How do you know if a product will be successful?"
Of course, there is no absolute answer, but the moment of truth comes when a customer selects your new product off the retail shelf and carries it to the check-out line. You see, you may have quick success with the development of your idea, and in licensing your invention, or selling your

product to wholesale buyers, but there's more. To be successful, your product has to do well in the retail arena. Those who buy your product once must be willing to purchase your product again. That's the measure of success! And unless you can discover the reason for any failure and make corrections, your product will die a certain death.

There is, however, a criteria used to forecast a potentially successful product. Let me give you six important statements that must be true if your invention is to become a reality.
- **One** - The product should be _____.
- **Two** - The product's _____ must be relatively _____.
- **Three** -The product's _____ must be _____.
- **Four** - The product's _____ should be _____.
- **Five** - The product's price should be _____ to _____ times its manufacturing cost.
- **Six** - The concept must have some type of _____. By this I mean patents, trademarks, copyrights, or licenses.

If your product concept falls within this criteria, your chances of success are greatly increased. Of course, there are still those exceptions to the rule, and not all successful products meet all six of these characteristics.

The second most-asked question is, "Assuming my product meets the success criteria, what are my chances of success?" I'm not sure I can really give you a scientific answer, but my experience has taught me that starting out, your chances of being successful are maybe one out of one hundred. If you fully develop your idea according to my successful development process, and endeavor to manufacture and market your product yourself, your chances may be one out of fifty. However, if you develop your idea and license it with a reputable company, your chances increase to two out of three. That is an endorsement for licensing, and I'll discuss this later under the section on licensing.

Let me say something at this point that I believe is very important for you to understand! Basically, I believe your best chance for success is directly proportionate to your willingness to develop your own idea.

In other words, generally speaking, the more willing you are to invest your time, energy and resources to develop your idea, the greater your chance for success, and the higher royalties you can demand. Of course, the lack of proper development adversely affects your chances. Believe me, this is one of the best kept secrets of successful inventors.

I have counseled many inventors who had wonderful product ideas, but that's all they had - an idea. Many times corporate managers' busy schedules make it impossible for them to have the necessary time for creative, inventive thinking. For this reason it is extremely difficult for them to think an invention through; to dream and imagine your product idea. They have to see everything in the development process with their eyes, and this means that you can't leave even the smallest detail to the imagination.

The proper development of your invention will increase your chances of being successful. (When I talk of success here, I'm referring to your financial rewards.) I don't believe an inventor can consider himself or herself to be successful until his invention is marketed, and he or she is making money. Now there are those exceptions when inventors invent for the good of humanity; however, for most of us one of the rewards of inventing is financial gain.

Quite frankly, I hope that the results of your hearing and acting on the information on this tape series, will be that you make money from your invention. Thomas Edison said, "Anything that won't sell, I don't want to invent."

I have used a specific development process guideline to successfully develop and license some of my inventions. I'm going to walk you through that guideline and note for you the order in which each segment should be undertaken. During your development process, you may be working on several items at one time. Keep in mind that what I'll be giving you will generally be the order in which each task should be completed. Each area will be discussed in detail later in this tape series, but for the time being, here is the brief outline.

The Development Process consists of:
- **One** - The Patent Disclosure.
- **Two** - The Patent Search.
- **Three** - Design Work .
- **Four** - A Prototype.
- **Five** - The Patent Application.
- **Six** - Name Selection, Logo & Trademark.
- **Seven** -Packaging Design and Prototype Package.
- **Eight** - Your Business Plan.

I believe that a person with average intelligence can successfully develop and license their own products. You, as the inventor of the product, are the lover of the product. How could anyone do a better job? Generally what you need for success in this type of business are these three simple elements:

First -A passion to see the development through. Webster's New Idea Dictionary describes passion as: love - the object of affection or enthusiasm. Your passion for the project provides the motivation to see it through to completion.

Second -The ability to control your day to day emotions. You must be patient. Product development takes a long time, and your progress will probably be slow. Two of Murphy's laws fit well here. "Nothing is as easy as it looks," and "Everything takes longer than you think."

Third -The ability to seek out the necessary assistance and know-how from others. Your greatest resources are other experienced inventors, consultants, universities, government agencies, inventor support groups, and trade publications like The Inventors' Digest. By tapping in to these resources, you'll minimize your mistakes by learning from others who have already made many costly mistakes.

Remember the famous words: "No man is an island, entire of itself; every man is a piece of the continent, a part of the main." Learn to benefit from the work already done by others.

INVENTION MARKETING FIRMS

It's been estimated that there are 300 "Idea Brokers" doing about $200 million of business each year working with some 200,000 hopeful inventors. These companies say that for a fee they will develop your idea, prepare your drawings, make a patent search, and license your product to a large company, and you will live happily ever after on those large royalty checks they promise.

Some of these companies are eager to convince you that your product has great potential, even if they know it really does not. The so called "Invention Marketing Service" is big business, and these individuals and companies will stop at nothing to get you to sign a contract or write that check. **Be cautious and aware of these unscrupulous companies**.

Many of the "invention marketing firms" advertise heavily on TV, radio, and in the advertisement section of magazines. Once you call them, mail their coupon in, or write, you will probably be contacted by a high pressure salesperson who will immediately assure you that your idea is a winner and you are going to be wealthy from your idea.

Their goal is to get you to agree to a **patent search** (which is the bait). If you agree to have them perform a patent search, they will be quick to assure you once again that your product is "a winner." The unsuspecting inventor assumes that the company would not go ahead with any plans if it was not possible to get a patent or if the concept did not have a good chance of success. This assumption is wrong!

Upon completion of the patent search, an invention marketing firm will normally mail you important looking letters encouraging you to agree to proceed with a marketing and direct mail campaign which costs thousands of dollars. These reports contain very little information that would entice a company to license your product. The reports, although they may cost as much as ten thousand dollars, are considered worthless by the very people that you want to impress - decision makers in charge of new product development in large companies. These reports are full of arbitrary figures and assumptions that one might arrive at after some light research at the library.

The sad fact is that the unsuspecting inventor thinks that he or she is developing the product by paying for these services. They are not! The most important areas of product development, like patents and prototypes, are almost never mentioned as part of the so called "product development campaign." The simple ten to twelve page marketing plans are mailed to company purchasing agents, sales managers and product managers. Guess where most of these marketing plans end up? In the trash can!

Another problem with this type of approach is that these plans may be a sales solicitation or public disclosure, and according to patent law, this disclosure may prohibit the inventor from ever filing for foreign patent protection. To make matters worse, if the product does seem promising, a large number of these "invention marketing companies" require the inventor to sign a contract giving the invention marketing firm twenty to thirty percent of the royalties the product may earn during the life of the patent.

Not all product development companies are of this nature. I believe there are some professional development companies and new product consultants who perform a needed service to inventors. They are staffed with men and women of integrity and purpose who strive to assist and educate their clients. Be cautious and don't be afraid to ask questions before making any commitments. To evaluate these companies, just ask these simple questions:

- Are you a member in good standing with the Better Business Bureau?
- Can you provide me with client references?
- Is it necessary to have a working prototype and a patent?

These three simple questions should do it.

If the representative of the invention marketing firm says, "No" to these questions, RUN (don't walk) for the door.

THINK ABOUT IT...

The process of getting from "idea" to "product" is one that requires planning, determination, wisdom and commitment. These questions serve as a springboard for documenting your response to what you are learning.

- Very briefly, state how you first thought of your invention idea.

_____

_____

_____

- Does your idea meet all six criteria for a successful invention?
    Yes ( ) No ( )
    If "no," which one(s) don't apply?

_____

_____

- List the three elements (personality traits) needed for successful product development.

_____

_____

- What does Mr. Fussell consider to the "the best kept secret of successful inventors?

_____

- List the 8 steps in the development process:

1 - _____   5 - _____
2 - _____   6 - _____
3 - _____   7 - _____
4 - _____   8 - _____

My Notes

"Left unprotected, your original idea may be lost in time."

If you intend to make a success out of new product development, you must start and maintain, from the moment of conception, a step-by-step activity diary of your invention.

There are two areas of invention protection you need to be concerned about. They are: (1) preliminary protection and (2) predominant protection. I'll discuss predominant protection which includes patent pending and patents later in this series, but right now let's look at the secret to preliminary protection.

There are four ways for you to protect your invention before you actually file for a patent:
- **One** - Maintain a dated _____ _____ on your invention.
- **Two** - File a _____ with the Patent and Trademark Office.
- **Three** - Use _____ Disclosure Agreements when talking to others about your invention.
- **Four** - Send _____ _____ after your meeting describing in detail the disclosures you made including all your discussions with people you met, dates and times.

However, remember that you do not have any statutory patent protection until your patent is actually issued by the U.S. Patent and Trademark Office.

Patent Work Diary

The first protection method I'd like to discuss is the Patent Work Diary. Few inventors carry out this simple documentation method. It's an accurate, dated diary of the original conception and development of the idea. Believe me, many times the courts and Patent and Trademark Office have accepted this type of evidence to prove that you are the original inventor.

Here are some good reasons why a patent work diary is important:

• First, maintaining a good record of your invention process allows you to know exactly where you are in that process and what remains to be done. This will help you avoid many costly mistakes.

• Second, it creates a _____ _____ to substantiate that you are the first and true inventor. If your invention is ever challenged, your complete diary will be the foundation of the legal protection for your idea.

• Third, it will convince others of the _____ of your invention. It is a "Mini Business Plan."

• Fourth, it _____, in one location, all of the information pertaining to your invention.

There are a number of important points to make regarding the use of a patent work diary. Follow these suggestions as you document the history of your invention.

• Always use a bound notebook for your patent work diary. This assures that no pages can be _____ or _____ _____.

• Number the pages in ink or buy a notebook that already has numbered pages.

• Make all of your drawings and sketches in ink.

• Include everything in your diary, no matter how rough or elementary.

• Describe your invention and how it works.

• Number the parts and explain each of them.

• Describe the _____ to be used in manufacturing.

• If you make a mistake, do not attempt to erase it. Just neatly line out those mistakes and make a dated note that details why the information was corrected.

• List the _____ you had along the development process and who you talked to, and the dates of each meeting.

Now, the following is **extremely important!**

• Major entries in your diary should be <u>signed, dated</u> and <u>witnessed</u>. Witnesses should be people who understand your invention and are capable of testifying on your behalf if a dispute over your invention should arise. **Do not** use family members or close friends.

More than once, a completed patent work diary has been submitted in court as evidence, and the diary has been accepted by the court to validate the original inventor's claim. You need to know, that even though you may have been granted a patent, it can be overturned by a federal court.

Consider this scenario. You work on an idea for a year, then file a patent application. It takes two years to get your patent. In the meantime, your product has become successful, and all of a sudden, out of the blue, you get notice of a law suit in the mail. Another person claims that he is the true and original inventor. The court must ascertain who had the concept first, and who developed the invention into a product. Your complete diary, if it goes back three years or more, may be the evidence necessary to win the suit that will allow you to retain your patent.

Disclosure Document Program

A second line of defense for protecting your idea is to register the conception and the date of your invention through the disclosure document program with the Patent and Trademark Office in Washington, D.C. This disclosure is accepted as evidence of the date of conception of the invention. The disclosure will be retained for two years, at which time it will be destroyed unless it is referred to in a separate letter in a related patent application. You should be aware that the two-year period that the Patent and Trademark Office will retain your idea, is nothing more than a grace period.

The Disclosure Document Program recognizes and establishes a date that you invented or conceived the concept. It does not give you any patent protection!

Also, you need to know that you cannot simply submit the disclosure document and do nothing. You must show that you are developing your concept during this period.

A fee of ten dollars must accompany the disclosure. The disclosure is limited to written matter or drawings not to exceed eight and a half by thirteen inches. However, photographs are acceptable. Each page should be numbered and the material should be of reproduction quality. The disclosure must be accompanied by a self-addressed, stamped envelope, and a duplicate copy, also signed by the inventor. The disclosure papers will be stamped with an identification number and returned with the reminder that the disclosure document may be relied upon only as evidence of the date of conception and that an application must be filed in order to provide patent protection.

Confidential Disclosure Agreements

When talking to any artist, engineer, prototype company, potential investor, or anyone else about your invention, don't walk away until you have a signed Confidential Disclosure Agreement. These Confidential Disclosures are agreements that simply say that the person and/or company signing the document agrees to hold all information about your invention in confidence, and will not use the idea for their own gain. A sample of this type of agreement is included in this workbook. It can also be found in several books that are presently available to inventors. Check your local library. A patent attorney can also provide you with a sample of this agreement.

Registered Letters

The final protection you have before the patent is filed, is the use of <u>registered letters</u>. Let's say the company you have contacted really seems to be interested in your product, but their legal department will not allow them to sign a non-disclosure. To make matters worse, before they will meet with you and evaluate your concept, they require you to sign a non-confidentiality agreement (which says you cannot hold them responsible for anything you show them). At this point I have used registered letters after the meeting, to show evidence of the fact that important information was disclosed to the company. Send the registered letter to the persons you met with, and keep a copy and the postal receipt. These registered letters are also useful tools to apply as you continue to sell yourself and keep your foot in the door for future opportunities.

One of the products that I invented (or I should say created) is a Christmas ornament. It's a unique, limited edition, hand painted, porcelain sports ornament figurine, made in the likeness of a professional athlete. After completing the development process, I researched prospective licensees and decided on the perfect candidate. Enesco Corporation is known around the world for marketing collectible, limited edition figurines. They even have a sports division.

When I called to set up an appointment for the big meeting, I was told that they did not sign Confidential Disclosure Agreements, and also they had been working on the concept of Sports Ornaments for over a year. However, after further discussions, the Vice President of

Licensing suggested that we still meet for discussions. She stated that "there may be some mutual ground here and some way we could work together."

At this point I had to make a judgment call. Enesco was already working on my product concept and had made it clear they were not going to sign a non-disclosure document. I made the decision to go through with the appointment and traveled to their corporate headquarters. I had a hunch that Enesco was sincerely interested in working with me, and I had a commitment for the sports licenses including Major League Baseball, the National Basketball Association and the National Football League. In addition to these, I had applied for copyrights for each ornament. Clearly, I had a degree of protection, and consequently I made the decision to proceed without a signed Confidential Disclosure Agreement.

It turned out that after Enesco saw the development progress I had made, and compared it to theirs, they agreed to scrap their program and license mine. (I had developed this product concept exactly as I will present the development process to you.)

Why was my development of the product so important to Enesco? They have experts on their staff who certainly could have reproduced my efforts. Here's the answer... TIME! This is the element that corporations do not have in abundance. Corporations need products that are ready to be introduced to market NOW. They may not have the time to develop the idea. Their shareholders and management are always pushing hard for more profits NOW - not next year.

So, just because a company will not sign your non-disclosure, does not necessarily mean you have to pass on that company. You make the final decision based on the interest expressed by the company, and your best hunch. You should know that although you may have a problem with some smaller companies, as a rule, large corporations are not going to rip you off. So don't be too paranoid.

Many deals between inventors and large corporations are still initiated on an old fashioned handshake.

In today's business climate, corporations have discovered that it is much easier to pay an inventor a royalty than go to court. Just look at what happened between the inventor of the intermittent windshield wiper concept and the automotive industry. This guy will probably be awarded over 100 million dollars in infringement damages before all the suits in this case are resolved.

MARKETING RESEARCH - PATENT SEARCH

Market Research You Can Perform

It is important to ascertain whether or not your invention is already on the market. You begin your research process by making a list of the different categories your product might be related to. These are called _____ _____. Search through different company and product catalogs. Take the time to personally go through stores and search for your product concept. Study thoroughly any product that you feel is closely related. Talk to experts in the field of your invention who know this type of product and/or the market. Ask if they have seen anything like your product, if they feel there is a need for your product. This is valuable market research.

Caution ! ! ! Most of the products that receive patents never make it to market. So, just because you can't find your product in the stores or in catalogs does not necessarily mean the idea has not been patented.

Another proven method of marketing research that you can perform is to attend _____ _____. Every year thousands of these shows are held in places all across the nation. Make a point to attend some of these shows. Most of them are free and all you need is a business card to get in. Some do charge for general admission but they are well worth the cost. Remember that the company employees manning the exhibit booths are there to sell products, not talk to inventors. If you do stop to ask questions, be considerate of their time and do not divulge too many details about your product. Also, never say that you have "invented a product." Say you are "working on a new product."

For the most part, you will be able to acquire a wealth of information just walking the aisles and noticing the products on display. Most shows hand out a show registry program and these have the names, addresses and telephone numbers of the participants, and these are generally most of the major players in that particular industry. Don't forget to pick up hand outs, literature and business cards.

Patent Searches

Since a patent is not always granted when an application is filed because the idea may have already been patented, many inventors attempt to make their own investigation before having a patent attorney perform a patent search or apply for a patent.

If you're interested in saving some money, you can conduct your own investigation in the search room of the Patent and Trademark Office and seventy one other libraries located throughout the U.S. which have been designated as "Patent Depository Libraries." Check your local telephone directory. There is no charge for the use of these facilities. The only cost is for any copies you might make. This is a wonderful learning experience and I think that every inventor should go through this exercise at least once.

You should begin your investigation by making a list of any patents that seem _____ to your concept. Read the patents thoroughly. They will tell you how the inventor came up with the idea, and how he or she made it work. Talk about training! This is some of the best product development training you will ever encounter.

Patent searches are also conducted by product development companies (which, by the way I do not recommend) and patent agents.

> *Here's my recommendation: Once you've completed your market research, and have performed a positive preliminary patent search, and you decide to pursue the development of your product, have a patent attorney conduct a formal patent search for you.*

A patent attorney usually conducts a more thorough search because he or she is more familiar with researching a wide range of product categories or fields of research. Also, they have a better understanding of how to evaluate the claims or lack of claims associated with the patents that are similar in nature to your concept.

I have also found that if you receive a positive letter from the patent attorney after the search, and in their opinion you may be entitled to a patent, your product concept now has some concrete credibility. This letter from the patent attorney may be very valuable if you need to raise capital and encourage others to help you in your development. Obviously, you will only have this official patent opinion if you include a patent attorney in your research process - a step that potentially can be very beneficial.

THINK ABOUT IT...

• Explain how you intend to document your invention in a "Patent Work Diary" as Mr. Fussell described. _____

_____

_____

• List here the people you will ask to serve as witnesses to your invention ideas.

_____

_____

_____

• What are the benefits of registering you idea through the disclosure document program?

_____

_____

- When should you have a patent attorney conduct a formal patent search?

  _____

  _____

  _____

- Describe the procedure you will follow when sending a registered letter.

  _____

  _____

  _____

- When researching whether your invention has already been patented or manufactured, which areas will you explore?

  _____

  _____

  _____

- Where will you research your preliminary patent search?

  _____

  _____

  _____

My Notes

DRAWINGS AND PROTOTYPES

There are three types of drawings associated with the new product development process. I would like to describe each of these so you won't become confused about which drawing we are discussing at different points in this material.

First, there is the <u>artist's concept drawing</u>. We will discuss this type of drawing in a moment. But first, let me explain the other two drawings which are necessary for you to complete the development process.

The second type of drawing is the <u>detailed engineering drawing</u>, which is sometimes referred to as a _____. These will be discussed a little later in this segment along with the third type of drawing referred to as the <u>patent drawing</u>. Patent drawings are necessary for both the utility and design patent applications. Patent attorneys usually work closely with several draftsman, and can arrange for your drawings to be completed. You, of course, have the right to hire a draftsman on your own; however, I believe it is in the best interest of your product and the patent to work through a patent attorney for the completion of patent drawings.

Now let me explain the <u>artist's concept drawing</u>. You should find a good artist to provide you with concept, black and white line drawings sometimes referred to as _____ or "concept" drawings. The line drawing is not an engineered blue print drawing. However, it does give you and the individuals you are working with a feel for the size of the product and how it will actually look. In other words, the drawing will give a better perspective of what you are trying to accomplish.

Once these drawings are completed, the artist's concept drawing will also help you believe that your idea can become a reality. It's difficult to see things with the mind's eye or the creative mind. I know that when I get an idea for a new product, I usually conduct a preliminary patent search, then have my artist complete a concept drawing. Looking at the drawing for the first time firmly plants the reality of the product in my mind.

The drawing provides a visual expression of an individual thought. This is the moment my invention comes to life in my conscious mind.

Search out an artist who has studied industrial design. Make the effort to hire the right industrial designer. This selection can prove to be money well spent. Large engineering companies use industrial designers to design your product, develop its features, package, field test and conduct market research. However, for most inventors who are just starting out, the cost for these services can be overwhelming .

Many good artists who work out of their home, have training and experience in industrial design. If you are lucky enough to locate the right artist, he or she can do just as good a job for you as design firms do for large corporations, while saving you thousands of dollars. Try your local <u>Small Business Development Center</u> or the <u>Small Business Administration</u> office. There is a good chance that they will have the name of a retired expert in the area. It is worth a try.

When you interview the artist, simply inquire if he or she has completed any industrial design training. This adds a special dimension to their abilities because simple artwork may not be enough to creatively enhance your concept.

PROTOTYPES

In all my years of conducting product development for my own products and working with other inventors, I have never seen an inventor successfully introduce his or her product or find a suitable licensee who did not have a _____ prototype. This is the heart of your product development efforts, so do not let anyone tell you that a prototype is unnecessary.

Let me say it again. You need a working prototype. This is truly one of the secrets of a successful inventor.

Prototyping can usually be divided into two stages. First, there usually is a <u>rough proto-type model</u>, and secondly, a more advanced <u>working model</u>. Many people sell themselves short when it comes to making a rough prototype of their invention. You probably have the ability to make a rough prototype right in your workshop or on your kitchen table. Some resources for the supplies you might need are the Yellow Pages, Thomas Register, trade, industrial, and arts and crafts magazines. There are also retail stores like craft and do-it-yourself centers where you might be able to purchase components and supplies to build your rough prototype model. I have seen several functional prototypes made out of cardboard, balsa wood and over-the-counter materials that are readily available at hardware stores.

There are two ways to develop prototypes. First, you can have an <u>industrial design house</u> take your entire project; or second, you can make the first generation prototype yourself, then engage a <u>small prototype shop</u> to do the second generation prototype. If you hire an industrial design firm, their efforts would include industrial design, drawings, prototype developing, building a production prototype and product testing. Now, when I refer to a "production prototype," I mean a prototype that looks <u>exactly</u> like your concept drawing - not similar, but <u>exactly</u>. It should perform <u>exactly</u> as a production model.

So many inventors schedule an appointment with a potential licensee, and go through their proposal, only to make a major mistake when they pull out a prototype that has not been fully developed.

Here comes the biggest "deal killer" I know of in the business. When making the presentation the inventor says, "Now this prototype is _____ _____like the finished production product will be..." At that very moment, the inventor loses all the credibility he or she might have gained and the presentation immediately takes a downward turn. **Do not make this mistake!**

> *If you do not have the prototype prepared and perfected, you really have no business being in front of a licensee prospect. This is a secret very few inventors know about, so use it to your advantage.*

With one of my inventions I visited a full service engineering company. After the firm signed a non-disclosure agreement, I disclosed my concept to a team of engineers. Later, I was quoted a price of $38,000 for the firm to provide their services. Now, this was a top notch, well known engineering firm with many references and accomplishments in the area of new product design and development. However, I simply could not afford this kind of expense. So, I decided to go in a different direction - to perform some of the work myself, and use more professional experience as it was needed.

I would like to take you through this process, step-by-step.

Step One - The Design Stage

I designed my product as best I could while concentrating mainly on function and performance, rather than aesthetics at this point. Of course, from the initial concept, I basically had an idea of how the product would look and function. Here I made pseudo engineering drawings which illustrated the dimensions and placement of components. This step cost me nothing more than my time.

Step Two - The Procurement Stage

I began the procurement of materials and components needed to build my first phase prototype. My search led me to wholesalers for Plexiglas and distributors of pumps. I even purchased a toy car so that I could use the on/off switch. The secret here is to improvise and use your creative abilities. This step cost me $300.00.

Step Three - The Assembly Stage.

I began this process after almost two months of careful search for the right materials and components. I assembled everything in my basement workshop, even though I'm no engineer. I made a lot of mistakes and tried a lot of materials that didn't work out. However, after three weeks, I had a working prototype. It really didn't look like much, but I can assure you that I had confidence in my prototype.

I remember coming out of the basement with prototype in hand. I went out to the carport and let the air out of two of the tires on my car. With mounting anticipation, I connected the air hose to the tire valve and pushed the on/off switch. The rush that came over me as I heard that handmade compressor run and watched as the tires were being inflated was incredible. The concept worked!!! I had a new product - an air compressor that did not need to be plugged into the cigarette lighter of the car because the compressor operated on a small twelve volt battery enclosed in the compressor housing; a product that would inflate the average car tire in about four minutes. After I inflated both tires, I plugged the recharge adapter into a receptacle and observed that it took only four hours to recharge the battery. This phase cost me nothing except my spare time.

Step Four - The Industrial Design Stage

I located an artist who had experience in industrial design. This person worked for an advertising agency but also worked out of his home at night and on weekends designing new products and providing concept drawings. My concept was a lightweight portable outside case that would be easy to handle and high-tech in appearance. The control panel would be designed so that the air gauge could be seen from different angles, the construction of the outside case needed to be high impact plastic, and free from excessive vibration. I got all that I expected and then some for two thousand dollars.

Step Five - The Advanced Engineering Stage

I found a small prototype shop that specialized in plastics. This company had great references and had provided plastic prototypes for companies like Coca-Cola and Black and Decker, but also seemed to thrive on small projects for inventors.

At this point, my goal was to have a prototype made that looked exactly (not closely) but exactly like the industrial design drawing.

The unit had to function under laboratory as well as field conditions. I knew that I needed a prototype to send to consumer testing laboratories as well as a model for field testing and another for a photographer's model. The three units cost me $2,100 and these prototypes held up as well as any of the production models we made later.

The total cost for the development of both prototype phases was approximately $4,400. The kind of assistance I described in the prototype development is probably available to you in your area. However, you'll need to search carefully for it.

• **<u>A note of caution here</u>** - If you obtain outside assistance with your prototype, have the company or individual you are working with, sign a _____ _____ _____.

If you want to build your prototype out of plastic, a good source to contact is a plastic tooling company. If your prototype needs to be engineered from metal, you may find that a machine shop would do a better job with the prototype. There are really good small prototype shops around; however, you really need to hunt for them. They specialize in producing machined and handmade prototypes.

One possible resource that provides excellent prototyping at a low cost is a university or engineering school. I have worked with several inventors who had prototypes constructed and evaluated by engineering students. Their only cost was for the materials. This kind of assistance would cost thousands of dollars if it were performed by professional engineering companies.

If you have your prototype developed by a machine shop, keep in mind that most machine shops fall into two categories - "Production shops," and "Job shops." Production shops usually manufacture several lines of parts or products in large quantities on a monthly contractual basis. Job shops specialize in one-of-a-kind jobs, and these shops employ trained I.E. operators who are experienced in Prototyping. These job shops are usually willing to devote the time necessary to develop a good working prototype at a reasonable price.

An important element in the prototype stage is field testing the prototype. When you think of product testing, you usually think of official consumer testing laboratories that test for product performance and product safety. I've had several of my inventions subjected to this type of testing. In addition to this type of testing, some products that have electrical components require UL testing or the equivalent agency testing in order to be marketed both in the United States and also in foreign countries.

You need to also be aware that some major mass merchandisers require that your product be tested by a consumer testing laboratory before they will issue you a purchase order. This testing will include operational tests as well as safety tests. The reason merchandisers require this testing is mainly for product liability insurance. If you need to locate a testing laboratory to test your product, you can call the American Council of Independent Laboratories in Washington, D.C. at (202) 877-5872. They will direct you to a facility near you.

However, there is another type of testing that is just as important. Fortunately you can do this testing yourself with a working prototype. I remember packing up my van with prototypes, literature and a card table. Off to the races I went as I intended to field test my invention at bicycle and motorcycle races. I was able to demonstrate to myself as well as hundreds of potential customers that the product functioned properly under field conditions. Not only that, but I also acquired some additional valuable market research and product improvement ideas at the same time.

While prototype testing, I discovered a major problem with my design and after talking to others and listening to how they would use my product, I was able to change the feature and improve the overall design and strengthen the claims for my patent.

ENGINEERING DRAWINGS

Once the prototype has been completed and tested to your satisfaction, and you are sure that there will be no further changes, you should have the machine shop or prototype shop produce three full sets of engineering drawings.

3-D cross-section dimensional blueprint drawings are necessary for accurate manufacturing pricing. The first thing a manufacturing company will require of you is a detailed and exact drawing before they will commit to a price. If your product requires plastic injection tooling, these drawings are vital. They are also necessary if special fixtures have to be built.

THINK ABOUT IT...

• To make my working prototype, I'll need the following materials:

_____

_____

• Mr. Fussell describes the "biggest deal-killer" as:

_____

_____

• Steps I need to take as I develop my prototype:

Design Stage: _____

_____

Procurement Stage: _____

_____

Assembly Stage: _____

_____

Industrial Design Stage: _____

_____

Advanced Engineering Stage: _____

_____

• What kind of product testing will I need to do with my prototype?

_____

_____

My Notes

What is a patent? A patent is a grant of a property right by the government to the inventor (or his heirs or assignees) for a term of seventeen years from the date the patent is granted. This term of seventeen years applies to a utility patent. A design patent is granted for fourteen years. <u>What is granted is not the right to make, use or sell, but the right to exclude others from making, using or selling the invention</u>. This year 175,000 patents will be issued and about half of them will be from foreign inventors.

Now, here is the million dollar question. Are patents Important? Here is the million dollar answer... You Bet! They are not always the perfect magic shield against knock-off artists, shady companies and individuals who are nothing more than thieves. But patents are all we have. As an inventor, if you intend to develop your idea, it is of utmost importance that you seek as much protection as possible.

> *If you intend to license your product, a patent is a must.*

Most companies will not even talk to you unless you have a patent, or at least have filed and have a patent application pending.

As a matter of interest, the United States Congress established the National Patent System in 1790. The first U.S. patent was issued on July 31, 1790 to Samuel Hopkins for a machine to make potash. The patent was signed by none other than George Washington.

However, the patent system was revised in 1836. Prior to this date, patents were not given a number. Patent Number One was issued in 1838 to Julius Hatch for his invention of a sewing machine. Also of interest is that on May 22, 1849 a patent was issued to Abraham Lincoln for his invention - a manner of buoying vessels.

Prior to 1880, the Patent Office required that inventors submit a working prototype model of their inventions.

However, the cost to maintain this collection of prototypes became too expensive, so the system was once again reformed. A lot of the earlier prototypes were destroyed in a fire in 1877. Today the National Museum of American History, Smithsonian Institute in Washington, D.C. currently holds nearly 10,000 patent models.

What can be patented? Anything a person "invents or discovers, any new and useful process, machine, manufacture or composition of matter, or any new and useful improvement may be patented." The patent law specifies that the subject matter must be useful.

There are three types of patents - Utility, Design and Plant patents (for those who have invented or discovered any distinct and new variety of plant.) However, for all practical purposes I'll discuss information pertaining mainly to utility and design patents.

In order for an invention to be patentable, it must be _____ and _____. The invention cannot be patented if the invention was known or used by others in this country, or patented or described in a printed publication in this or a foreign country. Nor can it be patented if the invention has been offered for public use, or on sale in this country for more than one year prior to the application for a patent. In other words, if the inventor offers the invention in a printed publication or uses the invention publicly or places it on sale, he or she must apply for a patent before one year passes. Otherwise, any rights to patent the invention will be lost.

Even if the subject matter sought to be patented is not exactly shown by the prior art, or involves one or more differences over the most similar thing already known, a patent may still be refused if the differences would have been considered obvious. For example, the substitution of one material for another, or changes in size are ordinarily not patentable features.

When a patent application has been filed and you receive official notification from the Patent and Trademark Office that the patent application was received and accepted, you may mark your product "Patent Pending" or "Patent Applied For." Once a patent is issued, you must mark the product with "Patented" and the number of the patent.

Applications for patents are not available to the public, and no information concerning them is released except on written authority of the applicant, his assignee or his attorney.

THE VALUE OF A PATENT ATTORNEY

Inventors have the right to file their own patents; however, once again I strongly recommend that you employ the skills of a patent attorney. The heart of a patent is in the claims of your invention. This determines the level of protection you can expect. Writing the claims requires skill and experience, and this is not a job for the novice. Let me tell you how important this is to your success. If you license your product concept, the stronger you make your product claims, the stronger the license agreement will be.

As with any profession, some patent attorneys are better than others. Also, some patent attorneys specialize in certain areas of inventions. I recently met a patent attorney who specializes in golf products. Find a patent attorney who specializes or has in-depth knowledge in the area of your invention. He is worth his weight in gold. You should take advantage of the free first consultation/meeting and make sure that the patent attorney you select is someone you can work with. Keep in mind that this will be a long-term relationship. I fully expect to enjoy a lifetime relationship with my patent attorney. He is very knowledgeable in the area of license agreements, and has been helpful in negotiating the license agreements I now have with my licensees, (some for as long as ten years). This is the type of professional relationship I recommend.

A word of advice - Start the relationship off right. Know what the patent attorney's fixed and hourly rates are so you won't have any major surprises when you receive your first bill for his or her service.

Here are two more important things concerning patents and patent attorney relationships.

• **Number one**: Remember the _____ _____ _____, and keep it holy. As mentioned earlier, you must file your patent application within one year from the day of a public disclosure of your invention. This includes any newspaper articles about your product, news releases or the sale or offering for sale of your product. Moreover, be aware that the moment you do any of the above, you may lose your right to file foreign patents. For this reason it is important to include your patent attorney as a major player in your product development strategy. Your attorney can advise you in regards to any complication that might adversely affect your plans. Strategy is everything! You, as the commander-in-chief, must have a nucleus of generals and advisors who can help you focus on the entire picture and see how it affects your new product development plans.

• **Number Two**: I have found that good patent attorneys usually make good licensing attorneys. At some point you will need this service, and if your patent attorney has been part of your development team, and has knowledge of what has transpired along the way, he can be of great benefit to you when it's time to negotiate a deal for the license.

WHAT HAPPENS AT THE PATENT OFFICE

Once your application has been filed in the Patent and Trademark Office, your attorney receives a filing receipt indicating the filing date and the serial number given to the patent application. Normally at this time, the Patent Office issues a "Foreign Filing License" which enables you to file foreign patent applications based upon your U.S. application. Once it is determined that your application meets the filing requirements, the application goes through a classification procedure. When it has been classified, your application is then routed to the proper Patent Office department for examination.

Once the application has been assigned to a specific patent examiner, it works its way to the top of the examiner's docket for formal examination and review. Inasmuch as all applications are examined in the order in which they are filed, it may be several months before any action is taken on your application. The time limit is controlled by the backlog of unexamined applications pending in the particular category unit to which your application has been assigned.

Every application is examined by a
_____ _____ _____who will make a formal, in-depth and thorough search among the prior patents and publications pertaining to this field. This search is similar to the preliminary patentability

search which is typically made for you by your patent attorney. However, the examiner's search will be more far reaching, as this search will include publications and foreign patents.

_____ _____are typically in the form of letters. Here the examiner will discuss formal matters pertaining to the application, which, in the opinion of the examiner, will need to be modified or changed to meet the requirements of the Patent Office. In addition, the examiner may well reject one or more of the claims of the patent application. Most patent applications go through two to three office actions. Once the office action has been received by your attorney, there must be a proper response filed within a time period set forth by the examiner in order to avoid abandonment of the application.

After the examiner receives the response to the first office action, the examiner will review the application and send a second office action. The second office action will be a second review of the application, and may be a notice of allowance, indicating that a patent will be granted, or it may repeat some or all of the previous grounds of rejection. Typically on the second or third office action, the examiner will make the action final, indicating that this is the final position of the Patent Office.

I've experienced this process first-hand while attempting to patent one of my inventions. The examiner had given my attorney his final position, and all my patent claims had been rejected. But I want to let you in on a little secret that most inventors don't know. <u>You can request a personal interview with the patent examiner</u>. If your reason is convincing enough to the examiner, and he or she agrees, you can have a meeting at the Patent Office with your attorney present to discuss why you feel your claims should be accepted. I was fortunate enough to get this kind of meeting when it seemed that obtaining a meaningful patent was impossible because of the position taken by the person who was assigned to examine my application.

During the meeting, I demonstrated my prototype and discussed the claims. My attorney then suggested that the claims might be reworded. Two months after the meeting, we received official notice that our new claims had been accepted and that I would receive my patent. I went on to develop the product which became a financial success for me.

Of course, there is no possible way to determine the amount of prosecution required during this process, and the costs are generally billed to the inventor in addition to the expenses for preparing the patent application.

If the examiner persists in the rejection of one or more claims of the application, or if the rejection has been made final, you may _____ the examiner's decision through the Patent and Trademark Office Board of Appeals.

THINK ABOUT IT...

• According to Mr. Fussell's definition, is your idea patentable?
  Why or why not?
  _____
  _____
  _____

• List the three types of patents.
  1 - _____
  2 - _____
  3 - _____

• Explain, in your own words, why you need a patent in order to license your idea.
  _____
  _____
  _____

• What is the most important part of the patent application?
  _____
  _____

• In your words, explain the "one year rule".
  _____
  _____
  _____

• At what point can you mark your product "Patent Pending"?
  _____
  _____

• Office actions are typically in the form of _____.

My Notes

My Notes

_____

_____

_____

_____

_____

_____

_____

_____

_____

_____

_____

_____

_____

_____

_____

_____

_____

_____

_____

_____

_____

_____

A Japanese proverb says . . . *"Life is for one generation; a good name is forever."*

Most inventors do not give much thought to product names, yet this is one of the secrets of successful product development. The right name and trademark can be just as important as your patent is to the long term strategy of developing your product idea. Patents can afford protection up to seventeen years, while trademarks are forever, as long as you maintain them. In addition to this, it's easier for the courts and U.S. Customs to police and give protection on trademarks than on patent infringements.

New product name research generally involves five dimensions. They are:
Connotations - the associated implications of the name.
Suitability - Does the name fit the product _____?
Pronunciation - Is the name easy to _____?
Memorability - Is the new product name easy to _____?
Familiarity - The new product name should not be too familiar to the consumer or be _____with another product name. The new product name should have a new sound when the product reaches the market.

The most important of these is the first one - name connotations. A new product name with strong positive associations can offer an extremely powerful market advantage.

Let me give you some examples of how I arrived at trademarks for several of my products.

OrnAroma

OrnAroma is a Christmas ornament that uses a heating element and plugs into a set of standard miniature Christmas tree lights. Inside the ornament is a fragrance cartridge that makes an artificial Christmas tree smell like a real, freshly cut Christmas tree.

Ornamotor

Ornamotor is a small motor that plugs into a standard set of miniature Christmas tree lights. The tiny motor hangs on the tree and rotates any Christmas ornament you hang on it.

Now do you better understand how to arrive at a trademark name?

> *The right name for your product should be suggestive, but never descriptive, and it should be easy for the consumer to remember.*

I suggest that if you are having a difficult time coming up with the right name, hire an advertising agency to help you. Most of these companies are extremely creative. They understand the new product name principle, and will present you with a list of names from which to select. Also, you can have this agency design a logo and trademark around the name.

WHY HAVE A TRADEMARK

A trademark may be a word, symbol, design or combination word and design, a slogan or even a distinctive sound which identifies and distinguishes the product or services of one party from those of another. If the mark is used to identify a service, it can be called a service mark. Normally, a trademark for goods appears on the product or on its packaging, while a service mark is most often displayed on advertising to identify the owner's services.

Unlike a copyright or patent, a trademark can last indefinitely if the mark continues to perform a source-indicating function. The term of federal trademark registration is ten years with renewal in ten year segments. However, between the fifth and sixth year after the date of the registration, the registrant must file an affidavit stating the mark is currently in use in commerce. If no affidavit is filed, the trademark is canceled.

Trademark rights arise from either (1) use of the mark or (2) a bona fide intention to use the mark along with the proper filing of a trademark registration. In addition, there are two types of filings for trademarks - state and federal. State common law protects the trademark rights as soon as the mark is used, but this common law protection is generally limited. Under this form of protection, you are allowed to use the designated ™ adjacent to the mark. A federal trademark registration is not required in order for that trademark to be used and protected; however, a federal trademark registration offers a greater means of protection and allows you to use the designated registered mark ® (the letter R in a circle) adjacent to the mark.

Before a trademark owner can file an application for a federal registration, the owner must either:
• **One** - use the mark on goods which are shipped or sold, or services which are rendered in interstate commerce or commerce between the U.S. and a foreign country, or
• **Two** - have a bona fide intention to use the mark.

Why is a trademark so important? Have you ever gone to a store to purchase a coffee maker and decided on a particular brand because you were more familiar with that name? Trademark identification can be a powerful tool in marketing, and an important business asset. The law allows the trademark owner to stop others from using the same or similar mark so that the consumer will not be confused as to the true source for the product. Under certain circumstances, if someone infringes on a product trademark, legally they can be made to pay damages to the trademark owner.

Let me explain it this way. In 1989, I licensed a product to a large company but insisted that they also market the product under my trademark. So the license agreement was written around both the patent and the trademark. This type of license agreement is much stronger and enforceable for the inventor, and I call this the "Secret Double Barrel License." A few years later, prior to the Christmas season, my licensee spent 2.5 million dollars advertising the product on national TV. My licensee (Noma International) developed the Ornamotion trademark and logo into a household name, and customers will recognize it for years to come. They relate it as the first product of its kind - the original product, and recognize it as a trusted name for quality and performance.

Now, ninety five percent of the license agreements are written to be enforceable for seventeen years (the life of the patent). But if the license includes a trademark, you can demand royalties for as long as the company uses your trademark, which could be indefinitely.

Now let's go a step further. Suppose a problem develops several years into your license agreement with your licensee and you wish to cancel the agreement. You may get the rights to manufacture and market your product back because the patent is yours. BUT if your licensee is marketing the product under its own trademark and trade names, then where does that leave you? You may face the loss of important name and product awareness - an extremely valuable element that often takes years to build. You might be in for another long process of rebuilding name and product awareness under a new trademark.

As mentioned earlier, trademarks are infinite in duration. However, they must be renewed accordingly. To do this, let me restate that you must prove the mark is being used in interstate commerce. You cannot simply sit on a trademark just to keep others from using it.

THE TRADEMARK APPLICATION

As with the patent application, I believe it is in the inventor's best interest to have a patent and trademark attorney file your federal trademark registration application. Remember, you may use the same depository libraries we talked about earlier to research trademarks that have already been registered by the Patent and Trademark Office. Performing formal research and filing federal trademarks can be tricky and it is best left to a professional. I have already been in a fight with one of the largest corporations in the United States over one of my registered trademarks. It was good to have a professional patent and trademark expert handle the concern on my behalf.

The Benefits of Filing a Federal Trademark Registration

• The filing date of the application for Federal Registration is a constructive date of first use of the mark in commerce. This gives you nationwide priority as to the date you started using the trademark.
• The registration gives you the right to sue in federal court for trademark infringement.
• The registration allows for recovery of profits, damages, costs and attorney's fees in a federal court infringement action.
• You are given the right to submit the trademark with U.S. Customs in order to stop the importation of goods bearing an infringing mark.
• The registration gives a basis for filing a trademark application in foreign countries.

The filing requirements consist of:
- **One** -   a written application form.
- **Two** -   a drawing (and by that I mean an artist's rendition) of the mark.
- **Three** - the required filing fee.
- **Four** -   three specimens showing actual use of the mark on or in connection with the goods or services.

A separate application must be filed for each trademark you are seeking. An applicant who alleges only a bona fide intention to use a trademark in commerce must make use of the mark in commerce before a registered mark can be issued. After use begins, the applicant must submit trademark specimens as proof of use. The application must be accompanied by a one hundred dollar fee per class of goods or services.

Copyrights

In some unusual situations your product may require you to file a copyright.

> *Copyrights are a form of protection provided by the laws of the United States to authors of literary, dramatic, musical, artistic and certain other intellectual works.*

For example, I created a unique line of collectible, limited edition sports ornaments. These could not be patented; however, I was able to secure the sports licenses from the National Football League and Major League Baseball. That allowed me to file a copyright on each ornament figurine produced. The two gave me adequate protection.

Copyrights are different from patents and trademarks. Copyrights protect one's expression, rather than the subject matter. They protect the original creation of authors and other creative people from those who may wish to copy their works. For works created or first published on or after January 1, 1978, the term of protection is the author's lifetime plus fifty years. Certain works made for hire carry a duration of seventy five to one hundred years from creation.

Copyrights are not handled by the Patent and Trademark Office. They are administered by the Library of Congress. Protection is available on both published and unpublished works. Everything from books to term papers are protected by the U.S. copyright laws.

To secure a copyright on your material, you simply use the copyright notice - (the letter "C" in a circle or the word "Copyright"), the year of the first publication and your name as the owner of the copyright. However, you can make a formal application with the Library of Congress which will give you a certificate of registration and the right to protect your copyright from infringement with the federal court if you obtain the registration within five years from the date your work was published.

A copyright, as patents and trademarks, is considered personal property, and some or all rights may be assigned to another. However, the assignment must be in writing. Copyrights may be willed to heirs and sold or licensed under a contract.

If you want to know whether or not you should seek a copyright for your product, I suggest that you consult your patent attorney who will be experienced in this area. The secret to remember concerning new product development is to "Use all the protection resources you can find. If your product concept is entitled to a patent, trademark and copyright, then use them all to your benefit."

PACKAGE DESIGN AND APPLICATION

Proper product packaging is just as important as any of the other product development steps. However, I rarely see an inventor who has gone this far in the development process. Remember my earlier statement, "The more you do, the higher the royalty?" This works most of the time, and this general rule includes developing product packaging.

There is just something about seeing your product in its final packaging that encourages you, and (in the eye of the potential licensee) adds worth and value to the product concept .

It is easier to negotiate your trademark into the license agreement if the packaging design and prototype packaging is completed, and the trademark is displayed on the package.

Remember, I stated in the beginning of this series that you can't leave anything to the imagination of large companies? They simply don't have any. I would suggest that you display your trademark on your prototype as well.

It has been said that you can't tell a book by its cover, but you can tell a product by its package. This is, at least, the thinking of many experts. You need to know that the decision to buy a new product is often strongly influenced by the ability of your product's packaging to attract attention and make the contents appealing.

A product's packaging is not just a container. Packaging should achieve the following:
  • It should _____ _____.
  • It should be a "point of purchase" means of advertising.
  • It should be a source of _____.
  • It should build _____ about the product inside.

The complicated part about this is that the packaging has to be able to achieve each of these in only a few seconds. Think about this. The new product package may be the only piece of advertising about your product a consumer ever sees.

I have found that there are a number of small product packaging prototype companies in most cities around the country. I've also successfully worked with some advertising companies to develop my product packaging. Once you select a packaging company, you'll want to explain to them the market you want to target. You'll also want to provide them with a prototype of your product. From your prototype they can take the necessary measurements and develop packaging for the product. They can also work up the necessary pricing for your manufacturing analysis and business plan.

The way a product is packaged is as much a science as the way in which the product is marketed. Choose very carefully the packaging company or advertising company that will help you with your project.

The final packaging design should be evaluated carefully since it could mean the difference between the success or failure of your product.

This is how critical a packaging concept can be.

An experienced buyer is a wonderful resource for evaluating your packaging. If your product is intended to be sold in the mass merchandising market, try to get an appointment with a buyer in this market and explain that your purpose is not to sell the product, but to get his or her professional opinion on your packaging. Most people like to be considered an expert and are willing to help. Maybe you know a friend who has a friend who is a buyer and would be willing to evaluate your packaging concept. Buyers generally know what catches a consumer's attention. Beware that no matter how good the packaging design firm may be, they can make mistakes and leave out important elements in your design. The buyer review is one of those invaluable "checks and balances" you can employ.

As I developed my first invention, I contracted with a packaging firm and had them design the package style for my product. Six months later, after I had shipped product all over the United States, buyers called my attention to the fact that several key ingredients were missing in the packaging design and suggested that I change the packaging because:

- **One** - The packaging did not get the consumer's attention.
- **Two** - The packaging did not properly describe the advantages of the product.

This was a costly mistake in terms of redesigning the packaging, but worse than that, I will never know how many sales were lost.

THINK ABOUT IT...

• The name you've selected for your product is:

_____

• How well does the name you've chosen for your invention fit Mr. Fussell's criteria?

_____

- • <u>Connotations</u>   _____
- • <u>Suitability</u>   _____
- • <u>Pronunciation</u>   _____
- • <u>Memorability</u>   _____
- • <u>Familiarity</u>   _____

> *A new product name with strong positive associations can offer an extremely powerful market advantage.*

• Explain Mr. Fussell's "Secret Double Barrel License."

_____

_____

_____

• What is the difference between a copyright and a patent?

_____

_____

_____

• Why is a trademark important?

_____

_____

• What are your initial thoughts on your package design?

_____

_____

My Notes

MANUFACTURING AND BUSINESS PLAN

When manufacturing a new product, there are two crucial questions to ask. "Can this product be made?" and "Can the product be sold at a profit?" The manufacturing part of your business plan should clearly answer both of these questions. Your manufacturing analysis should also address each of the following questions:

• Will your product be manufactured in the United States or overseas?
• How will the product be _____?
• What type of materials will be used?
• What is the target manufacturing _____?
• What kinds of _____ or special fixtures will be needed?
• Are the tolerances reasonable?
• Are there several sources for _____ _____?
• Can the product be packaged, stored and distributed easily?
• Are there alternative methods of manufacturing if some unseen problems in the process arise?
• If the product is to be manufactured off-shore, what are the _____ _____ and shipping costs?

If you don't have a lot of experience in this area, you may want to sit down with a manufacturing consultant and discuss the process. Probably the best source for locating manufacturing and engineering assistance is to contact a retired engineer. Here again, the Small Business Development Centers and the Small Business Administration can serve as a resource. They sometimes have a data bank of engineers and manufacturing experts who are looking for part time work on a per job basis. These experts won't charge the kind of fee you would pay if you employed the services of a large engineering firm, and retired engineers are generally very capable individuals.

If your product is electrical in nature, you will need a UL listing. Their Melville, New York office can be reached at (516) 271-6200. If you plan to market your product in Canada, you will also need a CSA listing. Their phone number is (416) 747-4000. You'll have to choose your materials carefully since UL and CSA have an approved list of materials which must be used when manufacturing certain products. Both agencies offer manuals which list these materials. However, an engineer who assists in your project will probably be familiar with these requirements.

BUSINESS PLAN AND RAISING CAPITAL

When a potential investor looks over your business plan, he or she should quickly and easily be able to identify:
- your <u>management plan</u>,
- your <u>product plan</u>
- and your _____ _____.

In addition, your business plan should answer an investor's questions even before they are asked. Questions like:
- How much money will I be able to make?
- How much money do I stand to possibly lose on this deal?
- How can I withdraw my investment and profit?
- Who are the people who have endorsed your business plan?
- Who are your other investors?

The best example I can give to demonstrate the importance of a well executed business plan is to describe my first experience in raising money for a new product. After inventing my first product and going through the development process (which was very close to the process I now use), I was in need of some additional capital for my project. I formed a corporation and decided to sell a portion of the shares. I have been constructing business plans for over twenty years; I have read many books, listened to tapes on the subject, and attended a seminar on "How to Prepare Successful Business Plans." I understood the importance of a business plan, so I set out to prepare my best business plan to-date.

<u>Here's a description of the business plan I presented</u>. It was assembled in a black three-ring binder, and each page of the presentation was placed in a clear plastic sheet protector. I believe I devoted at least a full week to the final preparations of the plan; but more importantly, I gave the project a month of careful thought. Generally when I am planning to construct a business plan, I think about the project for at least a month. I believe that during this time I am giving my subconscious mind the task of developing and unfolding the way the plan should be constructed. What I am saying is, when I sit down to type the business plan, the whole project has already taken shape in my mind.

A friend had given me the name of a wealthy business man in the community and suggested that I make an appointment to show him my prototype and business plan. During our meeting, I took the opportunity to demonstrate the prototype. Then he read most of my business plan. He believed in my product, and upon reading the business plan he realized the extent of my research and development, and understood why the additional money was needed. I will never forget that experience. He looked up at me and said, "You've answered all my questions before I could ask them." Then he opened his desk drawer and pulled out a checkbook and wrote me a check for $60,000.

Obviously, I believe in raising funds from private investors and friends; however, there are some down sides to this type of funding. But if you need small amounts of capital, it may be your only choice. I'll talk more about this a little later.

I look at business plans, how they relate to inventors, and the need to raise capital for new product development a little differently than most people. It's easy to get carried away studying break-even analysis, Pro Forma cash flow statements and other details that only a financial expert can understand. When developing a business plan, keep it as _____ as possible, especially if you are approaching a private investor. You need to anticipate and answer any questions a potential investor might have. You want to let the reader know that you clearly understand your quest and have a plan to achieve your goals.

> *The most important part of your business plan is to make sure you communicate the validity of your lifelong experience. You need to sell yourself first!*

When approaching banks, government guaranteed loans, research and development grants and venture-capital companies, you'll need a more formal type of business plan. In this type of business plan, people are everything. The resume section is the most important part of the plan. Bank financing, for most of us, is out of the question. Trust me, your bank is not going to loan you money on a high risk venture (like developing an invention) unless you have a proven track record from past ventures, and have adequate collateral.

Venture capital groups do, however, invest in inventor start-ups, but they often want controlling interest in the project. They will also insist on installing their own _____. Venture capital groups invest in companies with competent management teams not inventors. Actually, the inventor is secondary. It's no secret that the majority of inventors are incompetent when it comes to managing a business. If a venture capital group is going to invest major dollars in your product concept, they'll want to install an experienced professional who has been involved in previous successful new product launches. It normally takes 12 to 14 months to work through this type of approach.

Trust me! After the venture capital group gets through with you, you will be lucky to still own 20% of your product concept. Normally, venture capital groups don't even want to look at your business plan unless you need $250,000 and can show a 40 to 60 percent rate of return per annum compounded, which translates into 10 times their investment over 5 years.

Research and development grants are sometimes available to inventors from several different sources. I suggest that you contact your local representative for the <u>Small Business Administration (SBA)</u>. They should be able to provide you with information on what type of grants are presently available, and how to prepare grant proposals.

You may want to pursue securing a government guaranteed loan. Here again, your <u>SBA</u> representative should be able to advise you. I mentioned earlier that local <u>SBA</u> representatives are knowledgeable consultants in many areas of small business, and can offer you many important services, one of which is a source of information for entrepreneurs and inventors.

For most inventors, it's easier to secure funding from private investors such as doctors or other professionals you may already know. Or a friend may introduce you to a wealthy business man or woman. You want to be sure that the investment deal will be structured so that the investor realizes a savings on income tax. Also, be aware that your local <u>Industrial Development Authority</u> may have names of local private investors who might be interested in an investment opportunity that fits your project. Your local <u>Industrial Development Authority</u> is very interested in assisting the funding of your project if it can help increase local employment or benefit the community in some other way.

> *It is important for the plan to reflect the inventor's personality and enthusiasm.*

It's not necessary for you to follow any one outline entirely. Therefore, I like to be as creative with my business plans as I am with my new product concepts.

BUSINESS PLAN OUTLINE

A fully developed business plan should consist of the following:
- A title page listing the name of your business, address and the names of principals.
- An abstract, half-page summary of your plan.
- Corporate financial information, including shares of stock and net worth (which is your assets, minus liabilities.)
- Patent information, copies of letters from your patent attorney, patent pending information or patent document.
- Your marketing plan.
- Sales to-date.
- A forecast of future sales.
- Channels of distribution.
- Your marketing budget.
- Your production plan, current cost and future cost reductions.
- Product design and construction.
- A breakdown of material and labor, pricing and mark ups.
- Management resumes.
- Your financial plan and use of proceeds.
- Explain "What the investors get for their money."
- A cash flow budget showing anticipated income and expenses for two years.
- Manpower budget with salaries.
- General and administrative budgets.
- Product literature and pertinent articles.
- A binder or cover to put it all together.

Obviously, the business plan has to be adapted to your particular situation. Putting together a business plan is one of the best learning experiences you'll ever have. No matter how many times you've gone through the process, each time you will learn something new.

THINK ABOUT IT...

• What are your answers to Mr. Fussell's questions - "Can this product be made?" and "Can the product be sold at a profit?"

_____

_____

_____

• The Small Business Development Centers and the Small Business Administration can greatly assist inventors. Look up the location of the nearest SBA facility and write the address and phone number here. (SBDC information is included in this workbook.)

_____

_____

_____

• How do you determine whether you need a UL approval or not?

_____

_____

• Identify the major contents to your management plan.

_____

_____

  ...your product plan. _____

_____

_____

  ...your market plan. _____

_____

_____

• Your knowledge may be limited, but take a guess. How much of an investment do you think it will take to make your invention a reality? $_____ (Compare this with your actual cost.)

_____

_____

My Notes

My Notes

Four years ago I discovered a method for getting new products on the market, and with it, my thinking on new product introduction changed forever. With the first couple of products I invented, I followed the normal route of product introduction; the same route traveled by thousands of inventors and entrepreneurs each year. The generally accepted method of introducing a new product by an inventor or entrepreneur is laced with uncertainty, uncontrollable circumstances and extremely high financial risk.

> *The average inventor is unaware of an exciting alternative approach to marketing their product.*

With this approach, there is no need to be concerned with how to find adequate venture capital, how to start a manufacturing operation, how to find good employees or how to develop a profitable distribution network. By personality, an inventor is usually a solitary figure - not a team player. Creative individuals usually like to work alone. Most studies show that it is difficult for an inventor to build a successful company unless that person is willing to turn over the reins of management to someone who has experience with starting a business venture.

An inventor's driving desire is to profit from his or her invention, not necessarily to learn a new profession. Why should an airline pilot have to gain experience as a <u>manufacturing cost analysis expert</u>? Why should a printer be expected to build a successful distribution system?

For the majority of inventors, the answer is to license their invention to an established, successful company - one that has the resources to properly introduce their product. The introduction of a new product requires a major commitment of money and manpower. Studies show that the average new product requires one thousand man-hours before the product is ready to be introduced to the marketplace. This does not take into account the time you spend in concept development. Clearly, just one wrong decision or the omission of one step in the development process can mean the difference between success and failure.

So, the secret is for you to make a profit in this exciting adventure without turning your world upside down, and without risking the financial security you have worked so hard to establish.

Many inventors are guilty of committing a cardinal blunder. They may have come up with a great concept, so immediately quit their job with dreams of that million dollar check. After all, surely it's only months away! Most inventors who follow that path find themselves quickly disillusioned with the realization that they must continue to support their family and lifestyle and at the same time continue the development of their product. As an inventor, you are no different than any entrepreneur or business person. **You have to maintain cash flow**! Unfortunately, many inventors find themselves trapped in this dilemma too often. The penalty you pay for this choice is that you give up too much of your invention to venture capitalists or private investors by selling off large portions of your company in order to continue the development of your invention.

My own personal experience (which involves not only trial and error, but detailed study as well) and stories from hundreds of inventors, leave me with an overwhelming feeling that licensing is the secret. When you license your patented product instead of manufacturing and marketing it yourself, you appreciate the following advantages:

- You usually get to keep all or most of the _____ of your product.
- Your _____ remains low because you don't have manufacturing expenses or employees to hire.
- You don't have to hassle with _____ and _____ .
- You don't have the difficult task of developing a new marketing and distribution _____.
- Because the activities I've just mentioned are handled by someone else, you have the opportunity to develop _____ _____.
  Becoming a prolific inventor can be extremely rewarding.

You may think that you will make more money if you manufacture and market the product yourself, but let me explain why that's not usually the case. I happen to believe that for the average inventor (myself included) licensing will, in the long run, allow you the opportunity to make just as much money, with very little financial risk and only about one percent of the hassle.

The downside of licensing is that you give up control. However, there are advantages like not having to invest in manufacturing facilities, distribution and administration; no employees, and no accounts receivable and payable to keep track of, handle and be responsible for.

Let's assume that your product sells well. All you have to do is simply go to your mailbox for your check. Obviously, I am a firm believer that the average person has no business trying to manufacture or market their own product.

With my first invention, I tried to manufacture and market the product myself and l must admit, I really enjoyed it in the beginning. I incorporated a small manufacturing plant right in my garage. But my manufacturing experience was riddled with problems.

During the process my neighbors became angry with me, my house caught on fire, and over $300,000 worth of components which were built in Taiwan were delivered to me defective and unusable. This depleted my operating capital. At that time, I had a million dollars in components in my basement and could not ship one single product. Because of a flaw in the set up of our facilities, any quality control was extremely difficult to perform on a regular, dependable basis. I also suffered from a lack of qualified employees. These problems resulted in a large percentage of returns, and delayed our accounts receivable.

Now, years later, I am convinced that if I had developed this product as I have detailed in this tape series and workbook, and if I had licensed the invention with a reputable company, I would have made ten times the amount of money with only a fraction of the headache. Although this costly learning experience was wonderful for me, I'd rather have the money. Although I have made a lot of mistakes in product development, I can assure you that I have learned from these mistakes. These learning experiences have been instrumental in my recent success, and are also my motivating desire for the production of this tape series and workbook. If you are not making some mistakes, you're not attempting nor accomplishing very much. There's a saying, "He who has much to do will do something wrong."

HOW TO SELECT THE RIGHT LICENSEE

Corporations exist in order to make a profit. New, successful products equal profits. With this going for you, don't be afraid to approach large companies with your product idea. It takes no more time and effort to deal with a large company than it does to approach a small company. In addition, your chances of winning a successful deal are much greater with a large company. You see, large corporations usually have the engineering, manufacturing, marketing and advertising capabilities necessary to get your invention off the launching pad. It is important to note that twenty percent of the companies do eighty percent of the business.

Be aware that most likely your plans will be rejected as you begin your search for a licensee, so it's wise to plan ahead and prepare a list of as many prospective companies to contact as possible. I recently heard the story of an inventor who didn't give up, even after being rejected by forty six companies. You see, the forty seventh company he contacted, licensed his product and he made millions of dollars on royalties from the deal.

A critically important part of your business plan is the selection of the right licensee. It is so important that you'll need to take the necessary time to research each company you view as a potential candidate. Make sure the company you approach has the right marketing channel for your product. For example, don't waste their time by showing an automotive business your new computer product. Making an inappropriate presentation can cost you valuable time.

To streamline your expedition as you hunt for a potential partner, attempt to answer these questions:
• What does the company manufacture and what is the percentage of sales related to the whole product line?
• Are their sales seasonal or non-seasonal?
• How does the company market their product?
• Do they presently pay royalties to inventors?
• What kind of advertising budget does the company have?
• What are the company's manufacturing capabilities?
• Is the company involved in any legal proceedings?
• What is the company's area of distribution?
• Who are the officers of the company?
• What bank references can they offer?

If the industry into which you are introducing your product is unfamiliar to you, then go to your local library and begin some basic investigation and research. Let's say for example that you've invented a new type of air compressor. Look through the <u>Thomas Register of American Manufacturers</u> under the heading: "air compressors." Make a list of the companies that appear to have nationwide distribution. Research those companies in <u>Hoover's</u> or <u>Standard & Poor's Registry</u>. If you have the name of a particular company you want to approach and it is a public company, the best place to get information is the Security and Exchange Commission. Call them and request a "10K" form for that company. The "10K" form will reveal just about everything you need to know about the company.

Again, the information that is most important to you is the company's size; its annual sales, operating capital and net worth; names, addresses and telephone numbers of company officials, and other specific information discussed earlier. If the company is a public business, call them and request an annual report.

At this point, simply rank these companies according to size. I'd suggest that on a separate sheet of paper you list each company's profile. Include any valuable information you may have turned up during your research to assist in your decision making process. You will find an appropriate profile form in the back of this workbook.

Again, do not license your product with a small or newly started company if you have a choice. The reason? Their resources are limited, and that translates into a limited product introduction. Also, small companies find it extremely painful to pay an inventor his royalties if the sum becomes large due to successful or increased sales. You have a much greater likelihood of being paid by a larger company that has a broader financial base of operation. Let's look at one of my latest product introductions - the Ornamotor. Since the product operates from a set of Christmas tree lights, I began looking for a company not only in the Christmas market, but a company that manufactures and markets Christmas tree lights. I wanted to deal with a company with nationwide distribution, one that was financially sound, and had a history of working with outside inventors. After completing my research, I chose a company that offered all of the above, and was one of the largest suppliers of Christmas lights in the world. Our association has been mutually satisfying, and my research really paid off.

MAKING THE TELEPHONE APPROACH

You should know that large corporations are not likely to sign your confidential non-disclosure. They have to protect themselves from unsolicited outside disclosures. A lot of smaller companies will sign these agreements, but when contacting a large company, be prepared for a "No."

When an inventor approaches a corporation with a new product, the corporation has two major concerns:

• The corporation could very well be working on the same concept. If the corporation signs a confidential disclosure agreement to an outside inventor, it might jeopardize its own development program.

• The corporation doesn't want to pay for something that is available to others at no cost. The corporation wants to be assured that the inventor has a patent or patent pending. Without one or the other, it's almost impossible in today's business climate to get your foot in the door and present your new product idea.

It's very unlikely that you will ever get a corporation to pay you for an undeveloped idea.
YOU NEED THAT PATENT!

Now, don't get me wrong. Corporations do not want to ignore inventors. This is true because individuals invent twice as many new product concepts as large corporations. Individuals invented the Polaroid camera, digital computer, laser technology and the nuclear medical scanner. This list could go on for the next five minutes. Many corporations have been burned so many times by their working relationships with inventors. This makes it difficult for you and I to approach certain companies with a new concept.

Let me say that I do not believe that a large corporation will steal your concept on purpose. They have too much to lose. Also, if you have developed your concept according to my instructions in this series, you already have a patent or at least a patent pending. When you talk with representatives of large corporations, you need to rely on your patent protection, not on the confidential disclosure.

Although many inventors have successfully made their initial approach by correspondence, I have been more successful with the telephone, and in most situations believe it's your best bet.

This first contact can either "make you or break you." Almost every situation is different. However, there are some basics that fit every telephone approach.

First, think about your telephone approach several days before you actually make the call. Personally, I make the call and answer all the objections in my mind the day before I make the actual telephone approach. I know that getting the appointment requires imagination and strategy. It's a lot like playing poker on the telephone. It's fifty percent what you have, and fifty percent what they think you have.
Something else I try to keep in perspective is the realization that "I am doing the company a favor." If they license my idea, the company may be able to capitalize on a profitable concept, and the result will be an increase in sales and profits for them, and the possibility of new jobs for the community. I feel I have something of value to offer.

It is best to make the call very early in the morning between 7 a.m. and 9 a.m. on Tuesday, Wednesday or Thursday. On Monday your contact is generally too busy to devote the necessary time to you, and on Friday he or she is preoccupied with their plans for the weekend or already thinking about next week's work load.

When you call, do not simply introduce yourself as an inventor. Another secret! Most company officials think of inventors as weird unrealistic aliens from another planet. So, if you have a marketing degree, introduce yourself as a marketing expert and then say something like, "I have been working on a product that fits well into your product line."

Use your lifelong experiences to give you some credibility. If you are an engineer, introduce yourself as such and make the title of inventor secondary. When it comes to the use of the word "inventor," try substituting, "product developer" or something that describes your role without identifying you as a self-proclaimed "inventor." You want this person to understand that you are a person who is in touch with reality.

At this point in your approach, your goal is to "sell yourself." You want the company to "buy you as an individual." This is even more important than selling them on your invention.

- **STEP ONE** - Sell _____.
- **STEP TWO** - Sell your _____.
- **STEP THREE** - Sell the _____ _____.

You won't get to steps two and three if you are not successful with step one.

Let me take you through an actual telephone approach that I made with my licensee for the Ornamotor product.

I called the company at 7:45 a.m. their time, and asked the receptionist for the person in charge of "new product development". She immediately put me through to the <u>Director of Marketing</u>. I introduced myself as a consultant who had worked with Fortune 500 companies negotiating new product licenses. I told him that I had developed the most exciting new Christmas product to come along in forty years.

The voice on the other end of the telephone line curtly told me, "We have several new products on the drawing board and I don't think we have the time to develop any additional ideas this year." He was politely closing the door. Then I put my foot in the door and told him, "You probably misunderstood me. I do not have an idea." (You see, this is what most inventors call large companies with - ideas. That is a mistake!......)

I said, "I have a product that is ready to go to market. Everything from patent applications in ten countries, to trademarks and production prototypes, to packaging has been completed. There is nothing for you to do but introduce it into your line." That changed the whole mood of the conversation and was responsible for getting me the appointment to introduce my product in person.

THINK ABOUT IT...

- Explain in your own words why it is wiser to license your invention than to manufacture it yourself.

_____

_____

_____

- In this chapter, Mr. Fussell says that licensing is the secret. When you license your patented product instead of manufacturing and marketing it yourself, you appreciate the following advantages:

  - _____

  - _____

  - _____

  - _____

  - _____

- List the resources Mr. Fussell mentioned that offer helpful information when researching a potential licensee.

_____

_____

_____

- Use the space below to sketch out your approach when telephoning your selected contact.

_____

_____

_____

_____

_____

_____

_____

_____

_____

_____

_____

_____

_____

My Notes

Remember you are selling two things - yourself, and your new product concept. So when making your presentation, at all costs build your credibility with that company. If they don't perceive you as _____, they won't be interested in your concept - I don't care how good it may be or how much money it will make.

When I make a new product presentation to a company, I want the right people to be present at the meeting. I want their top executives who carry the decision making power for their company. Equally as important, I do not want any of the wrong people there. Let me explain further.

When I introduce a new product, I want meet with the Director of Marketing, Vice President of Marketing and President/CEO if possible; or other persons who are in charge of new product development. Be cautious of the title <u>New Product Review Manager</u>. These people are not decision makers. They make reports on new products and submit them to top management. I do not want this person submitting my product - I want to be the one submitting my idea.

Also, I do not want to meet with the Production Manager, the Chief Engineer or the Financial Manager. These people are interested only in details in manufacturing or cost and financial numbers. I do not want to discuss these at the first meeting. I simply want to sell my <u>new product concept</u>, generate excitement for this new additional product, and find a champion for my product. This is not a planning, engineering or production meeting. This is my one shot to sell my new product concept and I probably will not have a second chance.

There is another major reason to restrict the initial meeting to the real decision-makers. You see, the chief engineer or production manager will often resist what they view as an additional work load. They're not excited about additional products being added to their line, especially if the product being introduced was not invented from within the company. These are the guys who really have the NIH Syndrome. "_____ _____ _____!"

On the other hand, the Director of Marketing and the Vice President of Sales are very much interested in adding new products to the company's product line and increasing the company's profit margins. Company executives who are responsible for sales functions often participate in sales incentive bonuses, and you can bet they're interested in new products that will increase sales.

So, when I make the initial appointment, I request that all the company executives who may be involved in making decisions concerning new products be present at the meeting. I also request that the meeting be held early in the morning while everyone is fresh. It is easier to get their undivided attention at this time of the day. I also request that they reserve the boardroom or a meeting room we'll be using.

> *You need to present yourself and your product in a professional manner.*

Believe me, you don't want to be shoved into a crowded office where you have to deal with questions and comments as you attempt to set up what might be the most important presentation of your career. You'll find you have an important edge for the meeting if you have the opportunity to arrive at the company offices early and prepare by unpacking your prototype and other materials before anyone else arrives for the meeting.

If the company likes your product and the officers feel it's a good product mix for their present line, you're likely to be hit with this question. "If we go with your product, what kind of deal are you looking for?" Would you know what to say? Well you'd better prepare an answer beforehand, because this is how it happens! This is my answer. "I want X as a royalty on each piece sold, and I want X as a non-refundable advance payment against future royalties." I also say that if we can agree on these 2 issues, nothing will stand in our way of putting the deal together. The company spokesperson will normally say, "We will consider this and contact you after we have evaluated your proposal."

NEGOTIATING THE LICENSE AGREEMENT

> *"The Golden Rule for developing your licensing agreement is to negotiate a deal that you are satisfied with, and sign the agreement as soon as possible."*

When you get to this point, you'll need the services of a good, experienced attorney who deals with licensing agreements between inventors and large companies. A capable attorney will leave nothing to the imagination. But, keep in mind that your attorney should remain in the background as an adviser.

You don't want to involve your attorney in your day-to-day negotiations at this point, so here are some things you can do on your own. First of all, you are the only one who knows what kind of deal you want. What you should be looking for is a deal that is fair to both you and the company. Don't simply wait and hold out for all you can get. I have seen many inventors lose the whole game right here. The company may really want your product; however, I have never seen a company allow themselves to be jerked around by a greedy inventor and his or her attorney. Your potential licensee will probably, without notice, abruptly call the deal off if they feel this is happening. So, **know what you want**, and if you are lucky enough to get it , simply accept the deal and be content. Don't worry about whether or not you could have gotten more.

Let me tell you a story about an inventor in Atlanta, Georgia. His invention was a very unique and useful everyday tool. He obtained a utility patent with claims that gave him strong patent protection. As I understand it, this gentleman followed the development process as I have given it to you in this tape series and workbook. Upon completion of the development process, he had 50,000 pieces of his invention in his garage ready to be moved into the market place. It seemed up until this point he had done everything right - he had not contacted any buyers or distributors to solicit sales before the product was completely developed.

But now it was time to let the world know what he had. He made an appointment with a senior buyer at Sears and shortly after his meeting received a purchase order in the mail for 100,000 pieces at a hefty profit margin. Shortly before this meeting he had been contacted by a venture capital group on behalf of a foreign investor who saw his patent when it was published in the <u>Patent and Trademark Register</u> and had been negotiating a proposal to buy his patent. During the final negotiations the inventor agreed to sell his patent for one million dollars. At this point, although he had a nice purchase order, he was nearly out of money.

The story, as I understand it, is that on the day the inventor and his attorney met with the venture capital group and their attorney, there was a cashier's check for one million dollars laying on the conference table. At the beginning of what was to be the final settlement and signing of the documents, the inventor announced abruptly that he had changed his mind and he wanted two million dollars. There is no need for the details that followed.

Ten years later the tools are still in his garage (minus the freebies he has given to friends - by the way, I have one.) He is still trying to put together another deal which, may I add, will probably never happen.

> *Know what you want, and if you are lucky enough to get it simply accept the deal and be content.*

As I said earlier, know what you want, and if you are offered something close to that, something you can live with, do the deal. To put it another way, there is a saying in the stock market: Bulls and bears make money - pigs lose! Probably far more deals have been lost for inventors due to their own greed than any other contributing factor. Remember the winner's rule: "When you are winning, don't change the game." The secret here is to be content with a good deal.

As mentioned, I want to negotiate an _____ _____ into my license agreements. This allows me to recover some or all of the development costs up front. The companies that I negotiate with probably argue the hardest against this one area; however, I try to hold them to this. Your potential licensee will argue that they have to invest in manufacturing, marketing, distribution, etc. But you have an argument too - especially if you have fully developed your product idea according to the outline I have already given you. Do not give up too easy. Hold them to this point.

> *My experience has led me to firmly believe that if a company has made a financial commitment up-front, they are more likely to give your product a high priority.*

The other major thing you should fight for in your license agreement is a _____
_____ _____. In other words, you are guaranteed to make a specified amount regardless of how little of your product the licensee actually sells. You should know that twenty-five percent of the new products developed by large corporations never reach the market. They are killed for various reasons. Often, company objectives or market conditions change. Whatever the reason, even if thousands or millions of dollars are spent on the new product, top management may make a decision to kill the product.

My reason for giving you this information is to make you aware that just because your potential licensee promises great things for your product today, you can't be sure what changes tomorrow will bring.

Often the people you negotiate your deal with are transferred or leave the company, and you want to make sure that your product doesn't get caught up in company politics, and swept in a corner. If the company has made a financial commitment, you can bet that your project has a good chance of being kept alive.

The average royalty on a new product is around _____percent of wholesale, less shipping and uncollectable accounts. The higher the wholesale cost, the lower the royalty percentage seems to be. However, there are exceptions to the rule. <u>Once again, in product development, the more thoroughly you develop your idea, the more royalty percentage you can demand!</u> The highest royalties are from products that have been fully developed as we discussed earlier. I have seen royalties as high as one hundred percent of wholesale cost.

More than likely, the company you are negotiating with will want an exclusive right to your product. I personally feel that the exclusive right allows your licensee to do a little better job of allocating the funds for marketing and promotional expenses.

After a deal has been tentatively agreed upon by both parties, have your potential licensee submit the license agreement. Do not have your attorney prepare it. There are two reasons for this. First, you want to know the touchy areas, the hot buttons that concern the company the most. And, if the company prepares the agreement, you can bet that these concerns will stand out like a sore thumb. You (along with your attorney) will be able to conclude the deal with less time and aggravation if you are given this view of the other player's hand first. You don't want your deal to fall to pieces here over a few little legalities, incidentals or minor points. Secondly, let the company bear the _____ _____ to prepare the license agreement.

If your licensee will not prepare the agreement, then have your attorney prepare an agreement that would satisfy you, and then wait to see how it is received by the company.

A word in closing on this topic... _If the deal is not right for you, simply walk away. You will be glad you did later_. Don't commit to a bad deal just for the sake of being able to say you have licensed your invention. On the other hand, if the deal is right, get it signed, sealed and delivered as quickly as possible!

WHAT TO EXPECT AFTER SIGNING THE AGREEMENT

First of all, it may be six months to a year before your licensee completes the manufacturing start-up and begins distribution. That means it will be some time before you receive your first royalty check. Plan for this and don't quit your job yet!

Secondly here are some facts you should be aware of based on a study by the consulting firm of Booz-Allen & Hamilton, as condensed in Invention Management Magazine.

• Most inventors can not support themselves on royalties alone unless the product is extremely successful.
• Two thirds of the new products introduced by major corporations may be successful and of these, three-fourths will stay

on the market. However, half of these are modifications of existing products.
- By far, the most important reason companies license new products is technological advancements.
- By far, the biggest internal obstacle to making a new product successful is current business pressures on top management.
- Companies expect to double the number of new products they will introduce in the future.

Infringement of Patents

You need to be aware that under most license agreements you are responsible for protecting your patent in case there is infringement. Let me explain the meaning of patent infringement... Infringement of a patent exists if there is unauthorized making, using or selling of the patented invention within the United States during the term of the patent. If a patent is infringed upon, the inventor may sue for relief in a federal court. The inventor may ask the court for an injunction to prevent the continuation of the infringement and may also ask the court for an award for damages because of the infringement. Usually when an inventor sues for infringement the defendant raises the question of the validity of the patent which is then decided by the court. Remember I mentioned earlier in this series that any action of the Patent and Trademark Office can be overturned by a federal court.

Whether infringement has actually taken place is determined primarily by the language of the claims of the patent. If the product the defendant is making does not fall within the language of any of the claims of the patent, there is no infringement. Also, you need to know that if an inventor notifies anyone who is infringing on the patent or threatens suit, the one charged with infringement may start the suit in a federal court.

Develop a Product Line

Here's another secret... After securing the license deal for your invention, use your time and energy to develop a family of products around your patent. The key is developing _____ _____as well as your target market. The more you do in this area, the greater your income potential. Let me give you an example. After licensing the Ornamotor for the Christmas market, I discovered that the same motor would operate off fluorescent light fixtures used in drop ceilings. With this discovery, I doubled the potential markets for the product as well as earning potential because the product is currently selling in the Christmas and advertising markets.

Use your time and energy to develop a family of products around your patent and develop alternate markets.

Finally, you can expect an extraordinary feeling of accomplishment from your successful new product introduction. This is your opportunity to contribute to mankind. As Abraham Cowley wrote in the Seventeenth Century, "What shall I do to be forever known, and make the age to come my own?"

Oliver Wendell Holmes said, "The human mind, once stretched to a new idea, never goes back to its original dimensions."

You will never be the same after inventing your first product. The world around you seems to change. It is different. At least that is how it is for me. Your accomplishments become your special window to view life itself. But wait a minute, there is still more you can learn, more you can achieve, additional problems to solve and new inventions on the horizon.

Here are some things that will help you continue to develop your inventing abilities:
• **One** - In the Sixth Century BC, the philosopher Lao-tzu stressed the need for successful leadership by opposites. He wrote, "All behavior consists of opposites." You must learn to see things backward, inside out and upside down. This exercise will eventually become normal, everyday thinking that will help you solve problems that lead to new inventions.
• **Two** - Develop your creative place. Find a place you can let your creative powers work for you - a special place where you are comfortable. Mine is my office in my home. On the walls I have dozens of artists' renderings of my new product ideas, copies of patents and trademarks, articles I have had published and other things that mean a lot to me. This is my creative hole. Find yours!
• **Three** - Write down those ideas! Sometimes great ideas are invited by different techniques of brainstorming - others are uninvited. Whichever the case, you need to make a habit of having pen and paper close by. Write the ideas down before you forget them. Remember that capturing your idea on paper is the first step in developing a potential invention.

Through this tape series, you have been taught the fundamentals of new product development. I have shared some secrets concerning this process that I don't believe have ever been disclosed to the public. These ideas and fundamental steps will work if you will take the time to apply them. By changing my approach to new product development and incorporating these key points, I have been able to develop and license several of my inventions and most importantly ... I've made money.

You know, many times it's the simple details that make the difference between success and failure. These details I have given you, and I've held back nothing. You've got all the ammunition you need to load your big guns - SO DO IT!

I believe without reservation, I have supplied you with a million dollars worth of information. USE IT!

Good luck to you in your product development. As you use my development process, I hope that your dreams and secret desires concerning your invention become a reality.

THINK ABOUT IT...

• When making your presentation, you may be asked the question, "What kind of deal are you looking for?" How will you respond? Write your specific expectations here.

_____

_____

• What's the Golden Rule for developing your licensing agreement?

_____

• Two major things you should fight for in your license agreement are _____ and a _____ clause.

• How can you increase your earning power from your invention?

_____

• What is the most important reason a company chooses to license a new product?

_____

• Describe the meaning of "patent infringement."

_____

_____

• List the 3 things that will help you develop your inventing abilities.
   1) _____
   2) _____
   3) _____

My Notes

ANSWERS TO CHAPTER QUESTIONS

Chapter 1

1. easy to distribute
2. technology, simple
3. features, unique
4. benefits, obvious
5. three, five
6. protection

Chapter 2

1. work diary
2. disclosure
3. confidential
4. registered letters
5. legal record
6. worth
7. organizes
8. added, taken out
9. materials
10. appointments
11. research fields
12. trade shows
13. similar

Chapter 3

1. blueprint
2. descriptive
3. working
4. not exactly
5. confidential disclosure agreement

Chapter 4

1. new - unique
2. "One Year Rule"
3. Patent Office Examiner
4. office actions
5. appeal

Chapter 5

1. concept
2. pronounce
3. remember
4. confusing
5. attract attention
6. information
7. expectations

Chapter 6

1. manufactured
2. cost
3. tooling
4. raw materials
5. import duties
6. market plan
7. simple
8. management

Chapter 7

1. ownership
2. overhead
3. payables, receivables
4. network
5. new ideas
6. yourself
7. invention
8. business opportunity

Chapter 8

1. credible
2. "Not Invented Here"
3. initial payment
4. minimum royalty clause
5. five
6. financial cost
7. alternate markets

The following information is probably the most comprehensive ever provided for inventors. In particular, I strongly recommend the use of the Small Business Development Centers. Call the office nearest you. Introduce yourself and inquire about inventor and entrepreneur seminars and workshops that may be planned for the near future.

I believe that these agencies can provide you with more information and assistance than any other single resource in the country.

MOST OFTEN ASKED QUESTIONS ABOUT PATENTS, TRADEMARKS AND COPYRIGHTS.

Written by James A. Hinkle, Attorney at Law
Used by permission.

PATENTS

• WHAT IS A PATENT?

A patent is a grant to an inventor from the United States government to exclude others from making, using or selling the invention for a limited time.

• HOW IS A PATENT OBTAINED?

Patents are granted by the United States Patent and Trademark Office in Washington D.C. after a written application is filed with that office. A patent application describes the invention in detail and specifically states what the inventor believes is new and patentable. Each patent application is examined by the Office and if the invention is novel, useful and unobvious to a person of ordinary skill in the art, a patent is granted for the invention.

• ARE THERE DIFFERENT KINDS OF PATENTS?

Yes. The most common kinds are "utility patents" and "design patents."

A utility patent may be obtained for the utilitarian or functional nature of a machine, an article of manufacture, a composition of matter or a process.

A design patent may be obtained for the ornamental appearance of an article. A design patent protects only the physical appearance of an article and may not be used to exclude others from using the functional properties of the article.

In addition to these two types of patents, a plant patent may be obtained by anyone who develops or discovers and asexually reproduces a new variety of plant (i.e., tree, flower, etc.).

• WHAT IS THE DURATION OF A PATENT?

Utility patents expire seventeen years from the date the Patent and Trademark Office grants the patent, or sooner, if the required maintenance fees are not paid. Design patents expire fourteen years from the date of the grant. Patents cannot be renewed, so after the patent expires, an invention becomes public property and then may be used by anyone.

• ARE ALL INVENTIONS PATENTABLE?

No. An invention must fall into one of four classes of "patentable subject matter" as set forth in U.S. Patent Laws. The specific classes are: machines, articles of manufacture, compositions of matter and processes. An improvement to an invention included in these classes may also be patentable.

In addition to qualifying in one of the four classes, an invention must be "useful," "new" and "unobvious." A publication anywhere in the world which predates and describes the subject matter of your invention may prevent you from obtaining a patent on that invention.

• HOW CAN AN INVENTOR DETERMINE WHETHER AN INVENTION IS PATENTABLE?

A patentability search may be conducted to ascertain whether or not the proposed invention is patentably different from those disclosed in prior patents or publications ("prior art"). Therefore, it is advisable to conduct a patentability search within the files maintained by the U.S. Patent and Trademark Office in Washington D.C.

• IS AN INVENTOR REQUIRED TO CONDUCT A PATENTABILITY SEARCH ON AN INVENTION PRIOR TO APPLYING FOR A PATENT?

No. A patentability search is optional. However, many inventors desire to review the prior art before filing a patent application. For example, a patentability search may reveal a disclosure of a similar device in an earlier U.S. patent. Additionally, if the results of the search are unfavorable, then the inventor may save the expenses incurred preparing and filing an application or developing the invention.

• IS A PATENT REQUIRED ON AN INVENTION PRIOR TO THE INVENTOR SELLING IT?

No. However, only after a patent on your invention is granted by the U.S. Patent and Trademark Office will you have legal rights to prevent others from making, using or selling the invention.

• DOES A WORKING MODEL OF AN INVENTION HAVE TO BE CONSTRUCTED IN ORDER TO FILE A PATENT APPLICATION?

Not usually. However, if the Patent and Trademark Office determines that your invention is not operable, a model may be required to demonstrate that the device works as described in the application.

• WHAT DO THE TERMS "PATENT PENDING" AND "PATENT APPLIED FOR" MEAN?

These two terms are synonymous and mean that the inventor has filed a patent application that is "active" in the U.S. Patent and Trademark Office. The patent application remains "pending" until the Patent and Trademark Office makes its final determination either to deny or to grant a patent to the inventor.

• IS IT TOO LATE TO APPLY FOR A PATENT IF THE INVENTION IS ALREADY ON THE MARKET?

That depends on when the invention was first offered for sale or public use. Your invention cannot be patented if it was in public use or on sale in the U.S. or if the invention was described in a publication anywhere in the world more than one year prior to filing a patent application with the U.S. Patent and Trademark Office. When an invention can only be tested through extensive use, experimental use may not count when determining whether an invention has been "in use" for more than one year. Experimental use, however, is when an inventor is genuinely experimenting to determine whether or not he has a workable invention.

• CAN PROTECTION BE PRESERVED ON AN INVENTION BEFORE A PATENT IS APPLIED FOR?

Although you can have no patent protection until a U.S. patent is issued on your invention, the right to patent your invention may be preserved by establishing evidence of your inventive activities and by keeping your invention secret, while using diligence in perfecting your invention.

It is the first inventor who is entitled to a patent. While you are perfecting your invention (prior to filing your application), you can create evidence to prove your invention date. Generally, there are two ways of doing this.

The first method is to keep a written record of your invention which begins with its conception and includes additions or improvements. Each page of this written record should be signed and dated by you when you prepare it, should include sketches or drawings of your invention and should be signed and dated by one or more trustworthy witnesses who understand the invention but did not participate in its development.

The second method is to utilize the Patent and Trademark Office's Disclosure Document Protection Program whereby a written description of your invention will be dated and filed (for a small fee) and will be kept for a period of two years. The Disclosure Document does not take the place of filing a patent application, but serves only as evidence of your invention at the time of filing the Disclosure Document.

If you disclose your invention to another for commercial evaluation prior to filing a patent application, you should ask the other person to agree, in writing, not to disclose your invention to anyone else. Most businesses, however, will insist that you execute an agreement under which the company does not agree that your invention is a trade secret, requiring you to rely solely upon any patent rights you may have in the invention.

Therefore, it is advisable to contact a patent attorney in the early stages of the development of your invention in order to take the steps necessary to preserve your rights to your invention.

• IS IT NECESSARY TO HAVE A PATENT ATTORNEY TO FILE A PATENT APPLICATION?

An inventor has the right to prepare and file his own patent application, but an application is a highly technical document and a person unskilled in this specialized area of law may not be able to obtain a patent that fully protects the invention. For this reason, the inventor should seek the advice of a patent attorney or patent agent and have the attorney or agent prepare the patent application and communicate with the Patent and Trademark Office. Only attorneys or agents who have been admitted to practice before the U.S. Patent and Trademark Office may represent others in the filing and prosecution of patent applications. The patent attorney may also assist the inventor in other ways (e.g., conducting a patentability search on the invention).

• WHAT ARE THE OFFICIAL FEES FOR PATENT APPLICATIONS?

There are fees for filing an application, fees for issuance of the patent after it is granted and fees for maintaining a utility patent in force during its life, the amount of which is set by law. Individuals and small companies may pay half the set fee by filing proper sworn statements. If the invention is assigned or licensed to a large company, the full fees must be paid. Additionally, the U.S. Patent and Trademark Office may raise fees periodically.

• MAY A PATENT BE TRANSFERRED?

Like personal property, a patent (or patent application) can be assigned by a written instrument. A patent (or patent application) may also be conveyed by operation of law, may be bequeathed by will or passed under the law when a person dies without a will.

An inventor or anyone owning a patent (or patent application) may assign the patent to a third party or may grant a license under the patent to make, use or sell the device covered by the patent. To be valid against third parties, the assignment of a patent should be in writing and should be properly recorded in the U.S. Patent and Trademark Office.

TRADEMARKS

• WHAT IS A TRADEMARK?

A trademark or a service mark is a word, device or symbol used by an individual or business to identify its goods or services and to distinguish them from others.

Trademarks and service marks identify the goods and services as coming from a single source, and consumers rely upon these marks to locate goods and services with which they are familiar. Thus, the business utilizing a trademark builds "good will" or a reputation for quality that is immediately communicated to the consumer by the mark.

• HOW ARE TRADEMARK RIGHTS OBTAINED?

Trademark rights are acquired by using a mark of goods or services in commerce. County or state registration of a corporate or business name cannot create trademark rights in that name.

Under current law, one can file an application to register a mark in the United States Patent and Trademark Office based on a bona fide intent to use the mark. Such an "Intent To Use" application cannot proceed to registration until the mark is in use in commerce. Once the "Intent To Use" application matures into a registered mark, it will be granted national priority back to the original filing date of the application.

• HOW ARE TRADEMARKS PROTECTED?

State common law protects trademark rights as soon as the mark is used, but common law protection is generally limited to the geographic area of actual use.

State registration of trademarks used in Georgia may be obtained by filing an application with the Secretary of State for Georgia. After a trademark has been used in interstate commerce, or a bona fide intention to use the mark is formed, one may file an application with the U.S. Patent and Trademark Office. Although federal registration is not mandatory, federal registration gives notice to would-be innocent infringers throughout the entire U.S., in addition to providing other advantages and rights to the registrant.

• WHEN CAN "®" OR "™" BE USED WITH A TRADEMARK?

When federal trademark registration has been obtained, the familiar ® registration symbol should be used adjacent to the trademark or service mark to indicate the mark is registered. Prior to obtaining federal registration, the symbols "™" (for a trademark) or "sm" (for a service mark) can be used to indicate a claim of trademark or service mark rights in the mark.

• WHAT ARE THE RIGHTS OF A TRADEMARK OWNER?

The reputation or "good will" of a business is a valuable asset of the business. Therefore, the law allows the trademark owner to stop others from using the same or similar marks for similar or related goods or services where consumers would likely be confused as to the true source of the goods or services. And in the case of very famous trademarks, protection can even extend to unrelated goods. Furthermore, an infringer can be made to pay damages to the trademark owner under certain circumstances.

• WHAT ARE THE CRITERIA FOR SELECTING A STRONG TRADEMARK?

Words, slogans and drawings which merely describe characteristics or functions of goods are available for all to use and usually cannot be trademarks. The strongest marks are coined, arbitrary terms that have a descriptive meaning with respect to the product or service. Terms that suggest a product or a quality of the product can be protected as trademarks, but are typically not given as broad a scope of protection as are arbitrary terms.

If, however, someone has been the sole user of a heavily advertised descriptive term for a substantial period of time, the term may then develop a "secondary meaning," in that consumers view the term as an indication of the source of goods or services and be protectable as a trademark.

"Secondary meaning" can never exist for the generic or common name of a product such as "automobile" for cars. Trademark rights may be lost if the public adopts a trademark as a generic name for the product. This is exemplified in the former trademarks "escalator" for moving stairways and "aspirin" for pain pills.

Because selecting and protecting trademarks involve various legal requirements, an attorney familiar with trademark law should be consulted before a mark is first used.

• HOW CAN IT BE DETERMINED WHETHER A PARTICULAR MARK IS AVAILABLE?

A search should be conducted before a word is used as a trademark to see if the proposed trademark is likely to cause confusion with someone else's trademark. Trademark searches should cover, at least, the existing federal registrations and pending applications in the U.S. Patent and Trademark Office.

• MAY A TRADEMARK BE TRANSFERRED?

A trademark or trademark application is like personal property and, along with the good will of the business in which the mark is used, can be assigned or licensed by a written instrument. However, "Intent To Use" applications are not assignable until use in commerce begins and proof of use has been filed in the pending application in the U.S. Patent and Trademark Office. The assignment of a registered trademark or service mark should be promptly recorded in the U.S. Patent and Trademark Office.

COPYRIGHTS

• WHAT IS A COPYRIGHT?

A copyright is a federally granted right to protect the owner of original works of authorship from unauthorized copying or performance.

• HOW DO YOU OBTAIN A COPYRIGHT?

Although copyright arises automatically when the work is created, a notice of copyright may be placed on the work when published. For example, the copyright notice on a book or work of art would include: the word "Copyright" or the symbol ©, the year in which the work was first published, and the name of the copyright owner. An example of an appropriate notice is: Copyright 1992 Sam Doe. However, notice of copyright is not required for works published after March 1989, and the failure to give notice will not forfeit the copyright.

• WHEN DOES A COPYRIGHT NEED TO BE REGISTERED?

The copyright can be registered either before or after the work is published. The copyright must be registered before a suit for copyright infringement can be brought and, for maximum protection, should be registered within three months after first publication. If it is registered within five (5) years of first publication, some acts of publication without notice can be corrected.

• HOW DO YOU REGISTER A COPYRIGHT?

Registration is obtained by applying to the Copyright Office at the Library of Congress. This procedure requires filing an appropriate application with the Copyright Office, along with the required fee and copies of the work.

• WHAT TYPE OF THINGS CAN A COPYRIGHT PROTECT?

Copyright protection is designed to protect "original works of authorship." The protection of the author goes to the "form of expression" embodied in the work and not to the "concept" or "idea" which the "expression" embodies. Ideas, names, titles and unoriginal works cannot be copyrighted. Some common examples of authorship include writings such as books, computer programs, written articles, catalogs, advertising copy and compilations of information. Visual works such as graphic art, paintings, photographs, prints, maps, charts and technical drawings are also subject to copyright protection. Other examples of authorship include performing arts works in the nature of plays, songs, dance and motion pictures; and sound recordings such as phonograph records and tapes.

• WHEN DOES AN EMPLOYER OWN THE COPYRIGHT?

When a work is created by an employee within the scope of employment, the employer owns the copyright. The copyright in a commissioned work or a work created by an independent contractor, however, is generally owned by the creator of the work. If it is not clear whether a work is "commissioned" or "made for hire," the parties should initially enter into a written agreement as to the ownership of the copyright.

• WHAT IS THE DURATION OF A COPYRIGHT?

For works created or first published on or after January 1, 1978, the term of protection is the author's lifetime plus 50 years. The duration of a copyright on certain works, such as works made for hire, is 75 years from publication or 100 years from creation, whichever is shorter.

For works first published before 1978, the term of protection has been extended to a maximum of 75 years from first publication. Renewal, however, may be necessary to enjoy the full term.

• MAY A COPYRIGHT BE TRANSFERRED?

A copyright is like personal property and some or all rights may be assigned to another. The assignment, however, must be in writing. A copyright may also be conveyed by operation of law, may be bequeathed by a will or passed under the law when a person dies without a will, although there are rules which give certain designated heirs rights which may not be varied by a will.

An author or anyone who owns one or more of the rights in a copyright may transfer that right by a written contract. While the transfer may be recorded in the Copyright Office, it is not required to make the transfer valid. It may, however, be desirable to record the transfer in order to protect rights against third parties or to show legal title for enforcement of the copyright.

IMPORTANT CONTACTS

Information and Assistance on Patents, Trademarks and Copyrights

Patent and Trademark Office
U.S. Department of Commerce
Washington, DC 20231
(703) 557-4636

U.S. Copyright Office
Library of Congress
Washington, DC 20559
(202) 707-3000

Assistance in Enforcing Patents and Trademarks

U.S. International Trade Commission
Washington, DC 20436
(202) 482-2000

U.S. Customs Service
Department of the Treasury
511 NW Broadway
Portland, OR 97209
(503) 326-2871 or 1-800-BE-ALERT

Electrical and Safety Consumer Testing Agencies

Canadian Standards Association
178 Rexdale Blvd.
Rexdale (Toronto) Ontario, Canada M9W 1R3
(416) 747-4000

Underwriters Laboratories, Inc.
1285 Walt Whitman Road
Melville, NY 11747-3081
(516) 271-6200

Association of German Electrical Engineers (VDE)
Underwriters Laboratories, Inc.
12 Laboratory Drive, P.O. box 13995
Research Triangle Park, NC 27709
Tel. (919) 549-1545
Fax (919) 549-1842

ETL Albury
Manfield Park
Cranleigh, Surrey
Gu6 8PY U.K.
Tel. 011-44-483-268800
Fax 011-44-483-267579

Association of Independent Scientific, Engineering & Testing Firms (ACIL)
1629 K Street, NW, Suite 400
Washington, DC 20006
(202) 887-5872

Inventor Information and Assistance

Inventors' Digest Magazine
2132 E. Bijou Street
Colorado Springs, CO 80909
(719) 635-1916

Intellectual Property Oweners (IPO)
1255 Twenty-third Street, NW
Washington, DC 20037
(202) 466-2396

Superintendent of Documents
U.S. Government Printing Office
Washington, DC 20402
(202) 783-3238

Office of Technology Evaluatioin and Assessment
National Institute of Standards and Technology
Gaithersburg, MO 20899
(301) 975-2000

U.S. Department of Energy
Innovative Concepts Program
Forestal Building CE-50
1000 Independence Ave., SW
Washington, DC 20585
(202) 586-1478

National Innovation Workshops
Virginia Tech
2990 Telestar Court
Falls Church, VA 22042
(703) 698-6016

Japanese Trade Center
1221 Avenue of Americas
New York, NY 10010
(212) 997-0432
Atlanta # (404) 681-0600

Hong Kong Trade Development Council
154-2 World Trade Center
2050 Stemmons Freeway
Dallas, TX 75258
(214) 748-8162
Miami # (305) 577-0414

Nat. Society of Professional Engineers
1420 King Street
Alexandria, VA 22314
(703) 684-2800

Foundation for a Creative America
1755 Jefferson Davis Hwy #400
Arlington, VA 22202

The Wal-Mart Innovation Network
Center for Business Research
Southwest Missouri University
901 South National
Springfield, MO 65804
(417) 836-5667

National Council of Patent Law Assoc.
Crystal Plaza 3, Room 1D01
2021 Jefferson Davis Hwy.
Arlington, VA 22202
(703) 557-3341

German American Chamber of Comm.
666 Fifth Avenue
New York, NY 10103
(212) 974-8830
Atlanta # (404) 239-9494

China External Trade Center (Taiwan)
41 Madison Avenue
New York, NY 10020
(212) 730-4466

BONDED PATENT DRAFTSMEN

Mil-R Productions
2805 C Mt. Vernon Avenue
Alexandria, VA 22301
(703) 548-3879

Oblon & Spivak
1755 S. Jefferson Davis Hwy.
Crystal Square Five, Suite 400
Arlington, VA 22202
(703) 413-3000

Anthony L. Costantino
17300 Lafayette Drive
Olney, MD 20832
(301) 924-3491

Fleit, Jacobson, Cohn & Price
Jennifer Bldg.
400 7th Street, NW
Washington, DC 20004
(202) 638-6666

Ellsworth G. Jackson
101 Rittenhouse St., NW
Washington, DC 20011
(202) 726-0908

Litman Law Offices, Ltd.
P.O. Box 15035
Crystal City Station
Arlington, VA 22215-0035
(703) 412-1000

Patent Reproduction Co.
26 N St., SE
Washington, DC 20003
(202) 488-7096

J. A. Mortenson Patent Drafting
P.O. Box 518
Northeast, MD 21901
(410) 287-8669

Suzanne Nahmias
19559 Transhire Road
Gaithersburg, MD 20879
(301) 990-6014

Quinn Patent Drawing Service
9200 Hampton Overlook
Capitol Heights, MD 20743
(301) 808-4706

Edward J. Oliver
Oliver Patent Drafting Service
1205 Darlington Street
Forestville, MD 20747
(301) 336-0351

Mason, Fenwick & Larence
Suite 1000, 1225 1 Street, NW
Washington, DC 20005
(202) 289-1200

Robert MacCullum
Patent Drawing Services
13108 Engelwood Drive
Silver Springs, MD 20904
(301) 622-3940

Quality Patent Printing
701 South 23rd Street
Arlington, VA 22202
(703) 892-6212

PATENT AND TRADEMARK DEPOSITORY LIBRARIES

The Patent and Trademark Depository Libraries receive current issues of U.S. Patents and maintain collections of earlier issued patents and trademark information. These libraries are open to the public free of charge.

State	Name of Library	Telephone
Alabama	Auburn University Libraries	205 844-1738
	Birmingham Public Library	205 226-3600
Alaska	Anchorage Municipal Libraries	907 261-2975
Arizona	Tempe: Noble Library, Arizona State University	602 965-7607
Arkansas	Little Rock: Arkansas State Library	501 682-1527
California	Los Angeles Public Library	213 228-7000
	Sacramento: California State Library	916 654-0261
	San Diego Public Library	619 236-5800
	Sunnyvale: Patent Information Clearinghouse	408 730-7290
Colorado	Denver Public Library	303 640-8800
Connecticut	New Haven: Science Park Library	203 786-5447
Delaware	Newark: University of Delaware Library	302 831-2965
District of Columbia	Washington: Howard University Libraries	202 806-7252
Florida	Fort Lauderdale: Broward County Main Library	305 357-7377
	Miami-Dale Public Library	305 375-2665
	Orlando: University of Central Florida Libraries	407 823-2562
Georgia	Atlanta: Price Gilbert Memorial Library, Georgia Tech.	404 894-4508
Idaho	Moscow: University Of Idaho Library	208 885-6559
Illinois	Chicago Public Library	312 747-4300
	Springfield: Illinois State Library	217 782-2424
Indiana	Indianapolis-Marion County Public Library	317 269-1700
	West Lafayette: Purdue University Libraries	317 494-2873
Iowa	Des Moines: State Library of Iowa	515 283-4152
Kansas	Wichita: Ablah Library Wichita State University	316 689-3481
Kentucky	Louisville Free Public Library	502 574-1600
Louisiana	Baton Rouge: Troy Middleton Library, Louisiana State Univ.	504 388-3158
Maryland	College Park: University of Maryland Library	301 405-9257
Massachusetts	Amherst: Physical Sciences Library, University of Ma	413 545-0111
	Boston Public Library	617 536-5400
Michigan	Ann Arbor: University of Michigan Library	313 764-1817
	Big Rapids: Abigail S. Timme Library, Ferris State University	616 592-3602
	Detroit Public Library	313 833-1000
Minnesota	Minneapolis Public Library and Information Center	612 372-6500

State	Name of Library	Telephone
Missouri	Kansas City: Linda Hall Library	816 363-4600
	St. Louis Public Library	314 241-2288
Montana	Butte: Montana College Of Technology Library	406 496-4115
Nebraska	Lincoln: Engineering Library, University of Nebraska	402 472-7211
Nevada	Reno: University of Nevada-Reno Library	702 784-6508
New Hampshire	Durham: University of New Hampshire Library	603 862-1544
New Jersey	Newark Public Library	201 733-7800
Piscataway:	Library of Science and Medicine at Rutgers University	908 445-2895
New Mexico	Albuquerque: University of New Mexico Library	505 277-5761
New York	Albany: New York State University	518 473-4636
	Buffalo and Erie County Public Library	716 858-8900
	New York Public Library (The Research Library)	212 340-0849
North Carolina	Raleigh: D.H. Hill Library, N.C. State University	919 515-7426
Ohio	Cincinnati and Hamilton County, Public Library	513 369-6900
	Cleveland Public Library	216 623-2800
	Columbus: Ohio State University Libraries	614 292-3900
	Toledo/Lucas County Public Library	419 259-5200
Oklahoma	Stillwater: Oklahoma State University Library	405 744-7086
Oregon	Salem: Oregon State Library	503 378-6030
Pennsylvania	Philadelphia: The Free Library	215 686-5322
	Pittsburgh, Carnegie Library	412 622-3114
	University Park: Patee Library, Penn. State University	814 865-2112
Rhode Island	Providence Public Library	401 455-8000
South Carolina	Charleston: Medical University of South Carolina Library	803 863-7938
Tennessee	Memphis and Shelby County Public Library and Info. Center	901 725-8895
	Nashville: Vanderbilt University Library	615 322-2800
Texas	Austin: McKinney English Library, University of Texas, Austin	512 495-4500
	College Station: Sterling C. Evans Library, Texas A&M Univ.	409 845-5741
	Dallas Public Library	214 670-1400
	Houston: The Fondren Library, Rice University	713 527-4800
Utah	Salt Lake City: Marriott Library, University of Utah	801 581-6273
Virginia	Richmond: Virginia Commonwealth University Library	804 367-1109
Washington	Seattle: Engineering Library, University of Washington	206 543-9158
West Virginia	Morgantown: Evansdale Library, West Virginia University	304 293-0111
Wisconsin	Madison: University of Wisconsin-Madison	608 262-3193
	Milwaukee Public Library	414 286-3000

SMALL BUSINESS DEVELOPMENT CENTERS

ALABAMA

Univ. of Alabama at Birmingham - SBDC
Medical Towers Building
1717 11th Ave South, Suite 419
Birmingham, AL 35294-4410
205/934-7260   Fax: 205/934-7645

Univ of Alabama at Birmingham - SBDC
901 South 15th Street
MCJ Room 143
Birmingham, AL 35294-2060
205/934-6760

Auburn University - SBDC
226 Thach Hall
Auburn, AL 36849-5243
205/844-4220

University of North Alabama - SBDC
Box 5017 Keller Hall
Florence, AL 35632-0001
205/760-0001

Northeast Alabama Regional SBDC
AL A&M and The Univ. of AL at Huntsville
225 Church Stree NW
Huntsville, AL 35804-0343
205/535-2061

Jacksonville State University - SBDC
113 B Merrill Hall
Jacksonville, AL 36265
205/782-5271

Livingstone Universtiy - SBDC
Station 35
Livingstone, AL 35470
205/652-9661-439

University of South Alabama - SBDC
BMSB 101
Mobile, AL 36688
205/460-6004

Alabama State University - SBDC
915 South Jackson Street
Montgomery, AL 36195
205/269-1102

Troy State University - SBDC
Bibb Graves Room 107
Troy, AL 36082-0001
205/670-3771

University of Alabama - SBDC
Box 870396
400 N Martha Parham West
Tuscaloosa, AL 35487-0396
205/348-7621

University of Alabama
International Trade Center
Box 870396
400 N Martha Parham West
Tuscaloosa, AL 35487-0396
205/348-7011

ALASKA

University of AK Anchorage - SBDC
430 West Seventh Ave Suite 110
Anchorage, AK 99501
907/274-7232   Fax: 907/274-9524

University of Alaska Fairbanks - SBDC
510 Second Ave Suite 101
Fairbanks, AK 99701
907/456-1701   Fax: 907/456-1942

University of Alaska Southeast - SBDC
124 West Fifth Street
Juneau, AK 99801
907/463-3789   Fax: 907/463-5670

University of Alaska Mat-Su - SBDC
1801 Parks Highway Suite C-18
Wasilla, AK 99654
907/373-7232   Fax: 907/373-2560

ARIZONA

Arizona SBDC Network
9215 N Canyon Hwy
Phoenix, AZ 85021
602/943-2311   Fax: 602/371-8637

Northland Pioneer College - SBDC
P O Box 610
Holbrook, AZ   86025
602/537-2976

Mohave Community College - SBDC
1977 W Acoma Blvd
Lake Havasu City, AZ 86403
602/855-7812

SBDC - Gateway Community College
108 N 40th Street
Phoenix, AZ 85034
602/392-5220

Small Business Development Center
Rio Salado Community College
301 W Roosevelt Suite D
Phoenix, AZ   85003
602/238-9603

SBDC - Yavapai College
1100 E Sheldon Street
Prescott, AZ 86301
602/776-2373

Small Business Development Center
Eastern Arizona College
Thatcher, AZ 85552
602/428-7603

Small Business Development Center
Cochise College
901 N Colombo Room 411
Sierra Vista, AZ 85635
602/459-9778

Small Business Development Center
Pima Community College
655 North Alvernon #112
Tuscon, AZ 85711
602/884-6306

Small Business Development Center
Arizona Western College
W 24th St #121 Centruy Plaza
Yuma, AZ 85364
602/341-1650

ARKANSAS

Small Business Development Center
Univ of Arkansas at Little Rock
100 S Main, Suite 401
Little Rock, AR 72201
501/324-9043   Fax: 501/324-9049

Small Business Development Center
Henderson State University
1054 Huddleston
Arkadelphia, AR 71923
501/246-5511 (x327)

Arkansas College Business Division
Small Business Development Center
2400 Highland
Batesville, AR 72501
501/793-9813

Arkansas State Univ Beebe Branch
Small Business Development Center
Drawer H
Beebe, AR 72012-1008
501/882-6452 (x25)

University of Central Arkansas
Small Business Development Center
Burdick Business Administration Bldg
Conway, AR 72032
501/450-3190

University of AR at Fayetteville - SBDC
College of Business - BA 117
Fayetteville, AR 72701
501/575-5148

Phillips County Community College - SBDC
Economic Development Center
P O Box 785
Helena, AR 72342
501/338-6474 (x23)

Arkansas State University - SBDC
P O Drawer 2650
Jonesboro, AR 72467
501/972-3517

University of Arkansas, Monticello - SBDC
Rural Resource Development Center
P O Box 3486
Monticello, AR 71655
501/367-6811

Harding University - SBDC
Mabee School of Business Bldg
Blakeny & Center Streets
Searcy, AR 72143
501/268-6161 (x497)

CALIFORNIA

Small Business Development Center
801 K St 17th Floor Suite 1700
Sacramento, CA 95814
916/324-5068   Fax: 916/322-5084

Central Coast SBDC
6500 Soquel Drive
Aptos, CA 95003
408/479-6136   Fax: 408/479-5743

Sierra College SBDC
560 Wall Street Suite J
Auburn, CA 95603
916/885-5488   Fax: 916/781-0455

Weill Institute SBDC
2101 K Street Mall
Bakersfield, CA 93301
805/395-4148   Fax: 805/395-4134

Butte College Tri-County SBDC
260 Cohasset Avenue
Chico, CA 95926
916/895-9017   Fax: 916/895-9099

Southwestern College
SBDC & Int'l Trade Center
900 Otay Lakes Rd Bldg 1600
Chula Vista, CA 91910
619/482-6393   Fax: 619/482-6402

North Coast SBDC
882 H Street
Cresent City, CA 95531
707/464-2168   Fax: 707/465-3402

North Coast Satellite Center
408 7th Street Suite E
Eureka, CA 95501
707/445-9720

Central Valley SBDC
Cal-State University Fresno
2771 East Shaw Avenue
Fresno, CA 93740
209/278-4946   Fax: 209/373-7740

Gavilan College SBDC
5055 Santa Teresa Blvd
Gilroy, CA 95020
408/847-0373   Fax: 408/847-0393

SBDC of Lake / Mendocino County
P.O. Box 4550
Clearlake, CA 95422
707/263-6180   Fax: 707/263-0920

Greater San Diego Chamber of Commerce
Small Business Development Center
4275 Executive Square Ste 920
La Jolla, CA 92037
619/453-9388   Fax: 619/450-1997

Export SBDC of Southern CA
110 E 9th Suite A761
Los Angeles, CA 90079
213/892-1111   Fax: 213/892-8232

Merced Satellite Center
1632 "N" Street
Merced, CA 95340
209/385-7312   Fax: 209/383-4959

Valley Sierra SBDC
1012 Eleventh Street Ste 300
Modesto, CA 95354
209/521-6177   Fax: 209/521-9373

Napa Valley College SBDC
1556 First Street Suite 103
Napa, CA 94559
707/253-3210   Fax: 707/255-0972

Inland Empire SBDC
Inland Counties Legal Services, Inc.
1240 Palmyrita Ave Suite A
Riverside, CA 92507-1704
714/781-2345   Fax: 714/781-2353

East Bay SBDC
2201 Broadway Suite 814
Oakland, CA 94612
510/893-4114   Fax: 510/893-5532

Export Satellite Center
300 Esplanade Drive Suite 1010
Oxnard, CA 93030
805/981-4633

Eastern Los Angeles County
Small Business Development Center
363 S Park Ave Suite 105
Pomona, CA 91766
714/629-2247   Fax: 714/629-8310

Greater Sacremento SBDC
1787 Tribute Road Suite A
Sacremento, CA 95815
916/920-7949   Fax: 916/920-7940

Silicon Valley, San Mateo County
Small Business Development Center
111 N Market Street #150
San Jose, CA 95113
408/298-7694   Fax: 408/971-0680

Rancho Santiago SBDC
901 East Santa Ana Blvd Suite 108
Santa Ana, CA 92701
714/647-1172   Fax: 714/835-9008

San Joaquin Delta College - SBDC
814 N Hunter
Stockton, CA 95202
209/474-5089   Fax: 209/474-5605

Small Business Development Center
320 Campus Lane
Suisan, CA 94585
707/864-3382   Fax: 707/864-3386

Northern Los Angeles SBDC
14540 Victory Blvd Suite # 206
Van Nuys, CA 91411
818/373-7092   Fax: 818/373-7740

COLORADO

Office of Business Development
1625 Broadway Suite 1710
Denver, CO 80202
303/892-3809   Fax: 303/892-3848

Adams State College SBDC
Alamosa, CO 81102
719/589-7372   Fax: 719/589-7522

Community College of Aurora SBDC
16000 E Centretech PKwy#A201
Aurora, CO 80011-9036
303/360-4745   Fax: 303/360-4761

Pueblo Community College SBDC
402 Valley Road
Canon City, CO 81212
719/275-5335

SBDC Pikes Peak Community College
Colorado Springs Chamber of Commerce
P O Drawer C
Colorado Springs, CO 80901-3002
719/635-1551   Fax: 719/635-1571

Colorado NW Community College SBDC
50 Spruce Drive
Craig, CO 81625
303/824-7071   Fax: 303/824-3527

Delta Montrose Vocational School
Small Business Development Center
1765 US Highway 50
Delta, CO 81416
303/874-8772   Fax: 303/874-8796

Small Business Development Center
Community College of Denver
Greater Denver Chamber of Commerce
1445 Market Street
Denver, CO 80202
303/620-8076   Fax: 303/534-3200

Fort Lewis College SBDC
Miller Student Center Room 108
Durango, CO 81301
303/247-7188   Fax: 303/247-7620

Front Range Community College SBDC
P O Box 2397
Fort Collins, CO 80522
303/226-0881   Fax: 303/825-6819

Morgan Community College SBDC
300 Main Street
Fort Morgan, CO 80701
303/867-3351   Fax: 303/867-7580

SBDC Mesa State College
Grand Junction Business Incubator
304 W Main Street
Grand Junction, CO 81505-1606
303/248-7314   Fax: 303/241-0771

SBDC Aims Community College
Greeley/Weld Chamber of Commerce
1407 8th Ave
Greeley, CO 80631
303/352-3661   Fax: 303/352-3572

Red Rocks Community College SBDC
13300 W 6th Ave
Lakewood, CO 80401-5398
303/987-0710   Fax: 303/969-8039

Lamar Community College SBDC
2400 S Main
Lamar, CO 81052
719/336-8141   Fax: 719/336-2448

Small Business Development Center
Arapahoe Community College
South Metro Chamber of Commerce
7901 Southpark Plaza Suite 110
Littleton, CO 80120
303/795-5855   Fax: 303/795-7520

Pueblo Community College SBDC
900 W Orman Ave
Pueblo, CO 81004
719/549-3224   Fax: 719/546-2413

Morgan Community College SBDC
P O Box 28
Stratton, CO 80836
719/348-5596   Fax: 719/348-5887

SBDC Trinidad State Jr College
600 Prospect St Davis Bldg
Trinidad, CO 81082
719/846-5645   Fax: 719/846-5667

SBDC Colorado Mountain College
1310 Westhaven Drive
Vail, CO 81657
303/476-4040   Fax: 303/479-9212

Small Business Development Center
Front Range Communtiy College
3645 W 112th Ave
Westminster, CO 80030
303/460-1032   Fax: 303/466-1623

CONNECTICUT

University of Connecticut SBDC
Box U-41 Rm 422
368 Fairfield Road
Storrs, CT 06269-2041
203/486-4135   Fax: 203/486-1576

University of Bridgeport SBDC
230 Park Ave
Bridgeport, CT 06601
203/576-4000

Bridgeport Regional Business Council SBDC
10 Middle Street
Bridgeport, CT 06601
203/335-3800

University of Bridgeport SBDC
141 Linden Ave
Bridgeport, CT 06601
203/576-4538

SBDC Quinebaug Community College
742 Upper Maple Street
Danielson, CT 06239-1440
203/774-1130 (x309)

Small Business Development Center
Univesity of Connecticut
1084 Shennecossett Road
Administration Bldg Room 313
Groton, CT 06340-6097
203/449-1188

Small Business Development Center
Middlesex County Chamber of Commerce
393 Main Street
Middletown, CT 06457
203/344-2158

Small Business Development Center
Greater New Haven Chamber of Commerce
195 Church Street
New Haven, CT 06506
203/773-0782

Small Business Development Center
SACIA
One Landmark Square
Stamford, CT 06901
203/359-3220

University of Connecticut SBDC
Box U-41 Room 422
368 Fairfield Road
Storrs, CT 06269-204
203/486-4135   Fax: 203/486-1576

Greater Waterbury Chamber SBDC
83 Bank Street
Waterbury, CT 06702
203/757-0701

Small Business Development Center
University of Connecticut
1800 Asylum Ave
West Hartford, CT 06117
203/241-4986

Small Business Development Center
Eastern CT State University
83 Windham Street
Willimantic, CT 06226-2295
203/456-5349

DELEWARE

University of Delaware SBDC
Purnell Hall Suite 005
Newark DE 19716-2711
302/831-2747   Fax: 302/831-1423

DISTRICT OF COLUMBIA

Metropolitan Wasington SBDC
Howard University
2600 Sixth Street Room # 128
Washington, DC 20059
202/806-1550   Fax: 202/806-1777

George Washington University SBDC
Small Business Clinic
720 20th Street NW
Washington, DC 20052
202/994-7463   Fax: 202/994-4946

FLORIDA

Florida Atlantic University SBDC
500 Northwest 20th Street
Boca Raton, FL 33431-0991
407/338-2273

Small Business Development Center
46 SW First Ave
Dania, FL 33004
305/987-0100

Stetson University SBDC
602 N Woodland Blvd/PO Box 8417
Deland, FL 32720
407/734-1066

University of South Florida SBDC
W Thomas Howard Hall
Rooms 203 & 204
Fort Myers, FL 33907
813/489-9200

Indian River Community College SBDC
3209 Virginia Ave
Ft Pierce, FL 34981-5599
407/468-4700

University of West Florida SBDC
1170 MLK Jr Blvd Bldg 2/Room 250
Fort Walton Beach, FL 32548
904/863-6543

Central Florida Community College SBDC
P O Box 2518
Gainesville, FL 32602
904/377-5621

Florida Product Innovation Center
2622 NW 43rd Street Suite B-3
Gainesville, FL 32606

Florida International College SBDC
Trailer MO1 Tamiami Campus
Miami, FL 33199
305/554-2272

SBDC Florida International University
NE 151 & Biscayne Blvd
Academic Bldg #1 Room 350
Miami, FL 33181
305/940-5790

University of Central Florida SBDC
P O Box 25000 Bldg Ceba II
Orlando, FL 32816
407/823-5554

Palm Beach Community College SBDC
3160 PGA Blvd
Palm Beach Gardens, FL 33410
407/627-8706

Florida SBDC Network
University of West Florida
Bldg 76 Room 231
Pensacola, FL 32514
904/474-3016

University of West Florida SBDC
College of Business Bldg 8
Pensacola, FL 32514
904/474-2908

University of South Florida SBDC
830 First Street South Rm 113
St Petersburg, FL 33701
813/893-9529

Florida A&M University SBDC
P O Box 708
Commons Building Room 7
Tallahassee, FL 32307
904/599-3407

University of South Florida SBDC
College of Business Room 3331
Tampa, FL 33620
813/359-4292

GEORGIA

Southwest Georgia District SBDC
Business & Technology Center
230 S Jackson Street Suite 333
Albany, GA 31701-2885
912/430-4303

Morris Brown College SBDC
643 Martin Luther King Jr Drive NW
Atlanta, GA 30314
404/220-0201

Georgia State University SBDC
University Plaza Box 874
Atlanta, GA 30303-3083
404/651-3550

Augusta Small Business Development Ctr.
1061 Katherine Street
Augusta, GA 30910-6105
706/737-1790

Brunswick SBDC
1107 Fountain Lake Drive
Brunswick, GA 31525-3039
912/264-7343

Columbus SBDC
928 45th Street - North Bldg Room 523
Columbus, GA 31904-6572
404/649-7433

Dekalb SBDC/Chamber of Commerce
750 Commerce Drive
Decatur, GA 30030-2622
404/378-8000

Gainesville Small Business Development Center
455 Jesse Jewel Parkway Suite 302
Gainesville, GA 30501-4203
404/536-7984

Gwinnett Small Business Development Center
Gwinnett Technical Institute
1250 Atkinson Road
Lawrenceville, GA 30246
404/963-4902

Central Georgia District SBDC
P O Box 13212
Macon, GA 31208-3212
912/751-6592

Kennesaw State College SBDC
P O Box 444
Marietta, GA 30061
404/423-6450

Small Business Development Center
Clayton State College
P O Box 285
Morrow, GA 30260
404/961-3440

Small Business Development Center
Floyd College
P O Box 1864
Rome, GA 30162-1864
404/295-6326

Southeast Georgia District SBDC
450 Mall Blvd Suite H
Savannah, GA 31406-4824
912/356-2755

Statesboro Small Business Development Center
Landrum Center Box 8156
Statesboro, GA 30460
912/681-5194

Valdosta Small Business Development Center
Baytree Office Park
Suite 9, Baytree Road
Valdosta, GA 31602-2731
912/245-3738

HAWAII

Hawaii SBDC Network
University of Hawaii at Hilo
523 W Lanikaula Street
Hilo, HI 96720-4091
808/933-3515   Fax: 808/933-3683

Kauai Community College SBDC
8-1901 Kaumualii Highway
Lihue, HI 96766
808/245-8287

Maui Community College
Small Business Development Center
810 Kaahumanu Ave
Kahului, HI 96732
808/242-7646

IDAHO

Boise State University SBDC
1910 University Drive
Boise, ID 83725
208/385-1640   Fax: 208/385-3877

Panhandle Area Council
Small Business Development Center
11100 Airport Drive
Hayden, ID 83835
208/772-0587

Idaho State University SBDC
2300 N Yellowstone
Idaho Falls, ID 83401
208/523-1087

Lewis Clark State College SBDC
8th Avenue & 6th Street
Lewiston, ID 83501
208/799-2465

Small Business Development Center
Idaho State University
1651 Alvin Ricken Drive
Pocatello, ID 83201
208/232-4921

Small Business Development Center
Box 724
Sandpoint, ID 83864
208/263-4073

Small Business Development Center
P O Box 1238
Twin Falls, ID 83303-1238
208/733-9554 (477)

ILLINOIS

SBDC - Dept of Commerce & Affairs
620 East Adams Sreet 6th Floor
Springfield, IL 62701
217/524-5856   Fax: 217/785-6328

SBDC Aledo Chamber of Commerce
207 College Ave
Aledo, IL 61231
309/582-5373

Waubonsee Community College SBDC
Aurora Campus 5 E Galena Blvd.
Aurora, IL 60506
708/892-3334 (141)

Illinois State University SBDC
McClean County Chamber of Commerce
210 S East Street
Bloomington, IL 61702
309/829-6632

Small Business Development Center
Spoon River College RR #1
Canton, IL 61520
309/647-4645

Southern Illinois University - SBDC
College of Business Administration
Carbondale, IL 62901-6702
618/536-2424

Kaskaskia College SBDC
Shattuc Road
Centralia, IL 62801
618/532-2049

Parkland College SBDC
2400 W Bradley Ave
Champaign, IL 61821
217/351-2556

University Village Association- SBDC
925 S Loomis Street
Chicago, IL 60604
312/243-4045

Small Business Development Center
Chicago Area N'hood Devel. Organization
343 S Dearborn Street Ste 910
Chicago, IL 60604
312/939-7235

North River Commission - SBDC
4745 North Kedzie
Chicago, IL 60625
312/478-0202

Olive-Harvey Community College SBDC
10001 S Woodlawn Ave
Chicago, IL 60628
312/660-4839

Chicago State University SBDC
95th & King Dr - BHS601
Chicago, IL 60628
312/995-3944

SBDC - SE Chicago Develop. Commission
9204 S Commercial # 212
Chicago, IL 60617
312/731-8755

Women's Business Development Center
8 South Michigan Suite 400
Chicago, IL 60603
312/853-3477

Daley College SBDC
7500 S Pulaski Road
Chicago, IL 60652
312/838-4879

The Neighborhood Institute - SBDC
2255 East 75th Street
Chicago, IL 60649
312/933-2021

SBDC Greater N Pulaski Development Corp
4054 W North Ave
Chicago, IL 60639
312/384-2262

Cosmopolitan Chamber of Commerce SBDC
1326 S Michigan Ave
Chicago, IL 60605
312/786-0212

Small Business Development Center
Greater Westide Development Corp
3555 W Roosevelt Road
Chicago, IL 60624
312/762-2440

Little Village Chamber of Commerce/SBDC
3610 W 26th Street
Chicago, IL 60623
312/521-5387

Small Business Development Center
Latin/American Chamber of Commerce
2539 North Kedzie Suite 11
Chicago, IL 60647
312/252-5211

Small Business Development Center
Back of the Yards Neighborhood
1751 W 47th Street
Chicago, IL 60609
312/523-4419

SBDC - Park-Kenwood Development Corp.
5307 South Harper
Chicago, IL 60615
312/667-2610

Small Business Development Center
28 W North Street
Danville, IL 61832
217/442-7232

Small Business Development Center
Richland Community College
One College Park
Decatur, IL 62521
217/875-7200

North Illinois University Dept. of Mgt. SBDC
305 East Locust
Dekalb, IL 60115
815/753-1403

Sauk Valley Community College SBDC
173 IL Rt #2
Dixon, IL 61021
815/288-5605

College of Lake County SBDC
19351 West Washington
Grayslake, IL 60030
312/223-3633

Rend Lake Community College SBDC
Lower Level Student Center Rt #1
Ina, IL 62846
618/437-5321 (267)

Joliet Junior College SBDC
Renaissance Center Room 319
214 N Ottawa Street
Joliet, IL 60431
815/727-6544 (1313)

Blackhawk Community College SBDC
Business Resource Assistance Center
P O Box 489
Kewanee, IL 61443
309/852-3681

West Illinois University SBDC
216 Seal Hall
Macomb, IL 61455
309/298-1128

Small Business Development Center
Lake Land College
South Route # 45
Mattoon, IL 61938-9366
217/235-3131

Maple City Business/Technical Center
Small Business Development Center
620 South Main Street
Monmouth, IL 61462
309/734-4664

Small Business Development Center
Illinois Valley Community College
Bldg 11 Rt 1
Oglesby, IL 61348
815/223-1740

SBDC Procurement Assistance Center
233 East Chestnut Street
Olney, IL 62450
618/395-3011

Moraine Valley Community College
Small Business Development Center
Employment Training Center
10900 S 88th Ave
Palos Hills, IL 60465
708/974-5468

Bradley University SBDC
Lovelace Hall
Peoria, IL 61625
309/677-2309

Small Business Development Center
John Wood Community College
301 Oak
Quincy, IL 62301
217/228-5511

Small Business Development Center
Rock Valley College
1220 Rock Street Suite 180
Rockford, IL 61101-1437
815/968-4087

Lincoln Land Community College SBDC
509 W Capitol Suite 303
Springfield, IL 62704
217/492-4772

Shawnee College SBDC
Shawnee College Road
Ullin, IL 62992
618/634-9618

Governors State University SBDC
College of Business & Public Administration
University Park, IL 60466
708/534-3713

INDIANA

Indiana Small Business Development Ctr.
One North Capitol Suite 420
Indianapolis, IN 46204
317/264-6871   Fax: 317/264-3102

Bloomington Area SBDC
116 West 6th Street
Bloomington, IN 47404
812/339-8937   Fax: 812/336-0651

Columbus SBDC
4920 North Warren Drive
Columbus, IN 47203
812/372-6480   Fax: 812/372-0228

Southwestern Indiana
Small Business Development Center
100 NW Second Street Suite 200
Evansville, IN 47708
812/425-7232   Fax: 812/421-5883

Fort Wayne SBDC
1830 Wayne Trace
Fort Wayne, IN 46803
219/426-0040   Fax: 219/424-0024

Northlake SBDC
504 Broadway Suite 710
Gary, IN 46402
219/882-2000

Southern Indiana SBDC
1613 E Eighth Street
Jeffersonville, IN 47130
812/288-6451   Fax: 812/284-8314

Central Indiana SBDC
1317 West Michigan
Indianapolis, IN 46202
317/274-8200   Fax: 317/274-3997

Small Business Development Center
106 North Washington
Kokomo, IN 46903
317/457-5301   Fax: 317/452-4564

Greater Lafayette SBDC
122 N Third
Lafayette, IN 47901
317/742-2394   Fax: 317/742-6270

LaPorte SBDC
321 Lincolnway
LaPorte, IN 46350
219/326-7232

Southeastern Indiana
Small Business Development Center
301 East Main Street
Madison, IN 47250
812/265-3127   Fax: 812/265-2923

Northwest Indiana SBDC
8002 Utah Street
Merrillville, IN 46410
219/942-3496   Fax: 219/942-5806

East Central Indiana SBDC
401 South High Street
Muncie, IN 47308
317/284-8144   Fax: 317/741-5489

Richmond-Wayne County
Small Business Development Center
33 South 7 Street
Richmond, IN 47374
317/962-2887   Fax: 317/966-0882

South Bend SBDC
300 North Michigan
South Bend, IN 46601
219/282-4350   Fax: 219/282-4344

Terre Haute Area SBDC
Indiana State University
Terre Haute, IN 47809
812/237-7676   Fax: 812/237-7675

IOWA

Iowa State University
Small Business Development Center
111 Lynn Avenue
Ames, IA 50010
515/292-6351   Fax: 515/292-0020

Audubon SBDC Circle West Incubator
P O Box 204
Audubon, IA 50025
712/563-2623   Fax: 712/563-2301

University of Northern Iowa
Small Business Development Center
Suite 5 Business Bldg
Cedar Falls, IA 50614-0120
319/273-2696   Fax: 319/273-6830

Iowa Western Community College SBDC
2700 College Road Box 4C
Council Bluffs, IA 51502
712/325-3260   Fax: 712/325-3424

Southwestern Community College SBDC
1501 West Townline Road
Creston, IA 50801
515/782-4161   Fax: 515/782-4164

Eastern Iowa SBDC
Eastern Iowa Community College District
304 W Second Street
Davenport, IA 52801
319/322-4499   Fax: 319/322-3956

Drake University SBDC
Drake Business Center
Lower Level 210 Aliber Hall
Des Moines, IA 50311-4505
515/271-2655

Northeast Iowa SBDC
770 Town Clock Plaza
Dubuque, IA 52001
319/588-3350   Fax: 319/557-1591

Universsity of Iowa
SBDC Oakdale Campus
106 Tech Innovation Center
Iowa City, IA 52242
319/335-4057   Fax: 319/335-4489

Kirkwood Community College SBDC
2901 Tenth Ave
Marion, IA 52302
319/377-8256   Fax: 319/377-5667

North Iowa Area Community College SBDC
500 College Drive
Mason City, IA 50401
515/421-4342   Fax: 515/424-2011

Indian Hills Community College SBDC
525 Grandview Ave
Ottumwa, IA 52501
515/683-5127   Fax: 515/683-5263

Western Iowa Tech SBDC
5001 E Gordon Drive Box 265
Sioux City, IA 51102
712/274-6302   Fax: 712/274-6238

Iowa Lakes Community College SBDC
Gateway N Shopping Ctr N Hwy 71
Spencer, IA 51301
712/262-4213   Fax: 712/262-4047

Southeast Community College SBDC
Drawer F
West Burlington, IA 52655
319/752-2731   Fax: 319/752-4957

KANSAS

Kansas Small Business Development Center
Wichita State University
1845 Fairmont Campus, Box 148
Wichita, KS 67208
316/689-3193   Fax: 316/689-3647

Cowley County Community College SBDC
125 South 2nd
Arkansas City, KS 67005
316/442-0430 (251)

Butler County Community College SBDC
420 Walnut
Augusta, KS 67010
316/775-1124

Colby Community College SBDC
1255 South Range
Colby, KS 67701
913/462-3984 (239)

Dodge City Community College SBDC
2501 N 14th Ave
Dodge, City KS 67801
316/225-1321 (247)

Emporia State University SBDC
207 Cremer Hall
Emporia, KS 66801
316/343-5308

Garden City Community College SBDC
801 Campus Drive
Garden City, KS 67846
316/276-7611

Barton County Community College SBDC
115 Administration Bldg
Great Bend, KS 67530
316/792-2701 (267)

Hutchinson Community College SBDC
9th and Walnut #225
Hutchinson, KS 67501
316/665-4950

Small Business Development Center
Fort Hays State University
1301 Pine Street
Hays, KS 67601
913/628-5340

Kansas City Community College
Small Business Development Center
7250 State Ave
Kansas City, KS 66112
913/334-1100 (228)

Small Business Development Center
University of Kansas
734 Vermont Suite 104
Lawrence, KS 66044
913/843-8844

Seward County Community College
Small Business Development Center
1801 N Kansas
Liberal, KS 67901
316/624-1951 (148)

Small Business Development Center
Kansas State University
2323 Anderson Ave., Suite 100
Manhattan, KS 66506
913/532-5529

Small Business Development Center
Ottawa University
College Ave, Box 70
Ottawa, KS 66067
913/242-5200 (342)

Johnson County Community College
SBDC
CEC Bldg, Room 305I
Overland Park, KS 66210-1299
913/469-3878

Small Business Development Center
Pittsburg State University
Shirk Hall
Pittsburg, KS 66762
316/231-8267

Small Business Development Center
Pratt Community College SBDC
Highway 61
Pratt, KS 67124
316/672-5641

Small Business Development Center
Kansas College of Technology
2409 Scanlan Ave
Salina, KS 67401
913/825-0275 (445)

SBDC Washburn University of Topeka
School of Business
101 Henderson Learning Center
Topeka, KS 66621
913/295-6305

Small Business Development Center
Wichita State University
Brennan Hall 2nd Floor
(Campus Box 148)
Wichita, KS 672083
316/689-3193

KENTUCKY

Kentucky SBDC - University of Kentucky
225 Business & Economic Building
Lexington, KY 40506-0034
606/257-7668   Fax: 606/258-1907

Ashland SBDC
Boyd-Greenup Co. Chamber of Commerce
207 15th Street
Ashland, KY 41105-0830
606/329-8011

Bowling Green SBDC
Western Kentucky University
245 Grise Hall
Bowling Green, KY 42101
502/745-2901

Small Business Development Center
Southeast Community College
Room 113, Chrisman Hall
Cumberland, KY 40823
606/589-4514

Elizabethtown SBDC
University of Kentucky
238 West Dixie Ave
Elizabethtown, KY 42701
502/765-6737

Small Business Development Center
Northern Kentucky University
BEP Center 463
Highland Heights, KY 41009-0506
606/572-6524

Small Business Development Center
Hopkinsville
300 Hammond Drive
Hopkinsville, KY 42240
502/886-8666

Lexington Area SBDC
University of Kentucky
227 Business & Economics Building
Lexington, KY 40506-0034
606/257-7666

Small Business Development Center
Bellarmine College
School of Business, 2001 Newburg Rd
Louisville, KY 40205-0671
502/452-8282

University of Louisville SBDC
Center for Entrepreneurship & Technology
Rm 122 Burhans Hall - Shelby Campus
Louisville, KY 40292
502/588-7854

Morehead State University
Small Business Development Center
207 Downing Hall
Morehead, KY 40351
606/783-2895

Murray State University
Small Business Development Center
College of Business & Public Affairs
Murray, KY 42071
502/762-2856

Owensboro SBDC
3860 US Highway 60 West
Owensboro, KY 42301
502/926-8085

Pikeville SBDC
222 Hatcher Court
Pikeville, KY 41501
606/432-5848

South Central SBDC
East Kentucky University
107 W Mt Vernon Street
Somerset, KY 42501
606/678-5520

LOUISIANA

Louisiana Small Business Development Center
Northeast Louisiana University, Adm 2-57
Monroe, LA 71209-6435
318/342-5506   Fax: 318/342-5510

Captial SBDC - Southern University
9613 Interline Ave
Baton Rouge, LA 70809
504/922-0998

Southeastern LA University SBDC
College of Business Administration
SLU Station, Box 522
Hammond, LA 70402
504/549-3831

Acadiana SBDC
College of Business Administration
Box 43732
Lafayette, LA 70504
318/262-5344

McNeese State University SBDC
College of Business Administration
Lake Charles, LA 70609
318/475-5529

Northeast LA University SBDC
Administration Building 2-57
Monroe, LA 71209
318/342-5506

Northeast LA University SBDC
College of Business Administration
Monroe, LA 71209
318/342-1224

Northeast LA University SBDC
Monroe, LA 71209
318/342-5506

LA Electronic Assistance Program
Northeast LA University
College of Business Administration
Monroe, LA 71209
318/342-1215

Northwestern State University
Small Business Development Center
College of Business Administration
Natchitoches, LA 71497
318/357-5611

University of New Orleans
College of Business Administration
Lakefront Campus
New Orleans, LA 70148
504/286-6978

Loyola University SBDC
Box 134
New Orleans, LA 70118
504/286-6978

Southern University SBDC
College of Business Administration
New Orleans, LA 70126
504/286-5308

Small Business Development Center
Louisiana Tech University
Box 10318 Tech Station
Ruston, LA 71272-0046
318/257-3537

LSU-Shreveport SBDC
College of Business Adminstration
1 University Place
Shreveport, LA 71115
318/797-5144

Small Business Development Center
Nicholls State University
PO Box 2015
Thibodaux, LA 70310
504/448-4242

MAINE

Small Business Development Center
University of Southern Maine
96 Falmouth Street
Portland, ME 04103
207/780-4420   Fax: 207/780-4810

Small Business Development Center
Androscoggin Valley Council of Government
125 Manley Road
Auburn, ME 04210
207/783-9186

Eastern Maine
Development Corp. SBDC
1 Cumberland Place, Suite 300
Bangor, ME 04401-8520
207/942-6389

SBDC N Maine Reg. Planning Commission
2 Main Street
Caribou, ME 04736
207/498-8736

Small Business Development Center
University of Maine at Machias
Math & Science Building
Machias, ME 04654
207/255-3313

Small Business Development Center
Southern ME Reg. Planning Commission
Box Q, 255 Main Street
Sanford, ME 04073
207/342-0316

Small Business Development Center
 N Kennebec Reg. Planning Commission
7 Benton Ave
Winslow, ME 04901
207/873-0711

Small Business Development Center
Coastal Enterprises Inc.
Middle Street Box 268
Wiscasset, ME 04578
207/882-7552

MARYLAND

SBDC State Administration Office
Dept of Economic & Employment Develop.
217 East Redwood Street 10th Floor
Baltimore, MD 21202
410/333-6996   Fax: 410/333-6609

Central Region SBDC
1414 Key Highway
Baltimore, MD 21230
301/234-0505

Western Region SBDC
Three Commerce Drive
Cumberland, MD 21502
1-800-457-7233

SBDC National Business League
of Southern Maryland, Inc.
9201 Basil Court, Suite 115
Landover, MD 20785
301/772-3683   Fax: 301/772-0730

Eastern Shore Region SBDC
1101 Camden Ave
Salisbury, MD 21801
1-800-999-SBDC

Southern Region SBDC
235 Smallwood Village Center
Waldorf, MD 20602-1852
1-800-762-SBDC

MASSACHUSETTS

MSBDC Network State Office
Univ of MA School of Mgt. Room 205
Amherst, MA 01003
413/545-6301   Fax: 413/545-1273

University of Massachusetts/Boston SBDC
18 Tremont St
Boston, MA 02108-2301
617/287-7016

Metro Boston MA Regional Office
Boston College SBDC
Rahner House, 96 College Road
Chestnut Hill, MA 02167
617/552-4091

Captial Formation Service / Boston College
Rahner House, 96 College Road
Chestnut Hill, MA 02167
617/552-4091

Southeastern MA Region Office SBDC
University of Massachusetts/Dartmouth
200 Pocasset Street
Fall River, MA 02722
508/673-9783

Western MA Regional Office SBDC
University of Massachusetts/Amherst
101 State Street, Suite 424
Springfield, MA 01103
413/737-6712

Central MA Regional Office SBDC
Clark Univ. - Grad. School of Management
950 Main Street
Worcester, MA 01610
617/793-7615

North Shore Regional Office SBDC
Salem State College
197 Essex Street
Salem, MA 01970
508/741-6343

MICHIGAN

Michigan SBDC
2727 Second Ave
Detroit, MI 48201
313/577-4848   Fax: 313/577-4222

Michigan SBDC
Ottawa Co. Economic Development Office
6676 Lake Michigan Drive
Allendale, MI 49401
616/892-4120   Fax: 616/895-6670

Small Business Development Center
Huron County Economic Development Corp
Huron County Building, Room 303
Bad Axe, MI 48413
517/269-6431   Fax: 517/269-7221

MERRA
Specialty Business Develop. Center
P O Box 130500
Ann Arbor, MI 48113-0500
313/930-0034   Fax: 313/663-6622

Small Business Development Center
Kellogg Community College
450 North Ave
Battle Creek, MI 49017-3397
616/965-3023   Fax: 616/965-4133

Lake Michigan SBDC
Corporation & Community Development
2755 E Napier
Benton Harper, MI 49022-1899
616/927-3571 (247)   Fax: 616/927-4491

Small Business Development Center
Ferris State University
Alumni 226 / 901 S State Street
Big Rapids, MI 49307
616/592-3553   Fax: 616/592-3539

Wexford-Missaukee BDC
117 W Cass Street, Suite 1
Cadillac, MI 49601-0026
616/775-9776   Fax: 616/775-1440

Tuscola County Economic Delvelop. Corp. 194 N
State Street
Caro, MI 48723-1550
517/673-2849   Fax: 517/673-2517

Wayne State University
Small Business Development Center
School of Business Administration
2727 Second Ave
Detroit, MI 48201
313/577-4850   Fax: 313/577-8933

Comerica SBDC
8300 Van Dyke
Detroit, MI 48213
313/571-1040

NILAC-Marygrove College SBDC
8425 W McNichols
Detroit, MI 48221
313/345-2159   Fax: 313/864-6670

International Business Development Center
Michigan State University
6 Kellogg Center
East Lansing, MI 48824-1022
517/353-4336   Fax: 517/336-1009

1st Step Inc. Business Development Center
2415 14th Avenue South
Escanaba, MI 49829
906/786-9234   Fax: 906/786-4442

Genesee Economic Area Revitalization Inc. Small
Business Development Center
412 S Saginaw Street
Flint, MI 48502
313/238-7803   Fax: 313/238-7866

Small Business Development Center
Grand Rapids Community College
151 Fountain NE
Applied Tech Center
Grand Rapids, MI 49503
616/771-3600   Fax: 616/771-3605

Michigan Small Business Development Ctr.
Oceana Economic Development Corp
P O Box 168
Hart, MI 49420-0168
616/873-7141   Fax: 616/873-3710

Michigan Technology University
Bureau of Industrial Development
1400 Townsend Drive
Houghton, MI 49931
906/487-2470   Fax: 906/487-2858

MTU Forest Prod. Industry Assistance Ctr.
Bureau of Industrial Development
1700 College Ave
Houghton, MI 49931
906/487-2470   Fax: 906/487-2858

Livingston County SBDC
207 North Michigan Ave
PO Box 138
Howell, MI 48844
517/546-4020   Fax: 517/546-4115

Kalamazoo College SBDC
Stryker Center for Management Studies
1327 Academy Street
Kalamazoo, MI 49007
616/383-8602   Fax: 616/383-5663

Small Business Development Center
Lansing Community College
P O Box 40010
Lansing, MI 48901
517/483-1921   Fax: 517/483-9616

SBDC Lapeer Development Corporation
449 McCormick Drive
Lapeer, MI 48446
313/667-0080   Fax: 313/667-3541

Thumb Area County Growth Alliance
Small Business Development Center
3270 Wilson Street
Marlette, MI 48453
517/635-3561   Fax: 517/635-2230

Northern Economic Initiative Corporation
Small Business Development Center
1009 West Ridge Street
Marquette, MI 49855
906/228-5571   Fax: 906/228-5572

Michigan SBDC
Macomb Co. Business Assistance Network
115 South Groesbeck Hwy
Mt Clemens, MI 48043
313/469-5118   Fax: 313/469-6787

Small Business Development Center
Central Michigan University
256 Applied Business Studies Complex
Mt Pleasant, MI 48859
517/774-3270   Fax: 517/774-2372

Muskegon Economic Growth Dev. Alliance
349 W Webster Ave, Suite 104
Muskegon, MI 49443-1087
616/722-3751   Fax: 616/728-7251

SBDC Sanilac County Economic Growth
175 East Aitken Road
Peck, MI 48466
313/648-4311   Fax: 616/648-4617

Small Business Development Center
St Clair County Community College
323 Erie Street
Port Huron, MI 48061-5015
313/984-3881 (457)   Fax: 313/984-2852

Saginaw Future Inc SBDC
301 East Genesee, 4th Floor
Saginaw, MI 48607
517/754-8222   Fax: 517/754-1715

SBDC West Shore Community College
Business & Industrial Devel. Institute
3000 North Stiles Road
Scottville, MI 49454-0277
616/845-6211   Fax: 616/845-0207

Small Business Development Center
Montcalm Community College
2800 College Drive SW
Sidney, MI 48885
517/328-2111   Fax: 517/328-2950

Sterling Heights Area Chamber of Commerce
12900 Paul Road, Suite 110
Sterling Heights, MI 48313
313/731-5400

SBDC Warren, Center Line, Sterling Heights
Chamber of Commerce
40500 Van Dyke, #118
Sterling Heights, MI 48313
313/751-3939   Fax: 313/751-3995

Traverse Bay Economic Development Corp
202 E Grandview Pkwy
Traverse City, MI 49685-0387
616/946-1596   Fax: 616/946-2565

Greater Northwest Regional CDC
2200 Dendrinos Drive
Traverse City, MI 49685-0506
616/929-5000

Small Business Development Center
Northwest Michigan College
Center for Business & Industry
1701 E Front Street
Traverse City, MI 49685-0387
616/922-1105

Traverse City Chamber of Commerce BDC
202 E Grandview Pkwy
Traverse City, MI 49685-0387
616/947-5075

Walsh-O.C.C. Business Enterprise Dev. Ctr
340 E Big Beaver, Suite 100
Troy, MI 48083
313/689-4094   Fax: 313/689-4398

SBDC Saginaw Valley State University
Business & Industry Development Institute
2250 Pierce Road
University Center, MI 48710
517/790-4000   Fax: 517/790-1314

MINNESOTA

SBDC Dept. of Trade & Economic Devel.
121 7th Place East, #500
St Paul, MN 55101-2118
612/297-5770   Fax: 612/296-1290

SBDC Bemidji State University
1500 Birchmont Drive, NE
Bemidji, MN 56601
218/755-2750

SBDC Normandale Community College
9700 France Ave., South
Bloomington, MN 55431
612/832-6395

SBDC Brainerd Technical Institute
300 Quince Street
Brainerd, MN 56401
218/828-5302

Center for Economic Development
University of Minnesota
10 University Drive, 150 SBE
Duluth, MN 55811
218/726-8761

Small Business Development Center
Faribault City Hall
208 NW First
Faribault, MN 55021
507/334-2222

Small Business Development Center
19 NE Third Street
Grand Rapids, MN 55744
218/327-2241

SBDC Hibbing Community College
1515 East 25th Street
Hibbing, MN 55746
218/262-6700

Small Business Development Center
Rainy River Community College
Highway 11 & 71
International Falls, MN 56649
218/285-2255

Small Business Development Center
Mankato State University
Box 145
Mankato, MN 56001
507/389-1648

SBDC Southwest State University
ST # 105
Marshall, MN 56258
507/537-7386

SBDC Minnesota Project Innovation
111 3rd Ave South, Suite 100
Minneapolis, MN 55401
612/338-3280

Small Business Development Center
Moorhead State University
Box 303 - MSU
Moorhead, MN 56563-0001
218/236-2289

SBDC Pine Technical Intstitute
1000 Fourth Street
Pine City, MN 55063
612/629-7340

SBDC Hennepin Technical College
1820 North Zenium Lane
Plymouth, MN 55441
612/559-3535 (7153)

SBDC Red Wing Technical Institute
Highway 58 at Pioneer Road
Red Wing, MN 55066
612/388-4079

SBDC Rochester Community College
Highway 14 East
851 30th Ave SE
Rochester, MN 55904
507/285-7536

SBDC Dakota County Technical Institute
1300 145th Street East
Rosemount, MN 55068
612/423-8262

SBDC St. Cloud State University
Business Resource Center
St. Cloud, MN 56304
612/255-4842

Small Business Development Center
University of St. Thomas
23 Empire Drive
S.t Paul, MN 55103
612/223-8663

SBDC Thief River Falls Technical Institute
Highway One East
Thief River Falls, MN 56701
218/681-5424

SBDC Mesabi Community College
905 West Chestnut
Virginia, MN 55792
218/749-7729

Small Business Development Center
Wadena Technical Institute
222 Second Street, SE
Wadena, MN 56482
218/631-2674

NE Metro Technical Institute SBDC
3300 Century Ave North
White Bear Lake, MN 55110
612/779-5764

Small Business Development Center
Winona State University
Winona, MN 55987
507/457-5088

MISSISSIPPI

SBDC
Old Chemistry Bldg, Suite 216
University, MS 38677
601/232-5001   Fax: 601/232-5650

SBDC Delta State University
P O Box 3235 DSU
Cleveland, MS 38733
601/846-4236` Fax: 601/846-4443

SBDC Mississippi Delta Community College
1656 East Union Street
Greenville, MS 38702
601/378-8183

Small Business Development Center
Pearl River Community College
Route 9, Box 1325
Hattiesburg, MS 39401
601/544-0030   Fax: 601/544-0032

Small Business Development Center
MS Dept of Economic/Community Development
P O Box 849
Jackson, MS 39205
601/359-3179   Fax: 601/359-2832

SBDC Jackson State University
Suite A1 Jackson Enterprise Center
931 Highway 80 West
Jackson, MS 39204
601/968-2795   Fax: 601/968-2358

SBDC University of Soutern Mississippi
USM Gulf Park Campus
Long Beach, MS 39560
601/865-4578   Fax: 601/865-4544

Small Business Development Center
Meridian Community College
5500 Highway 19 North
Meridian, MS 39307
601/482-7445   Fax: 601/482-5803

Small Business Development Center
Mississippi State University
P O Box 5288, McCool Hall, Rm 229
Mississippi State, MS 39762
601/325-8684   Fax: 601/325-8686

Small Business Development Center
Copiah-Lincoln Community College
Natchez Campus
Natchez, MS 39120
601/445-5254   Fax: 601/446-9967

Small Business Development Center
Itawamba Community College
653 Eason Blvd
Tupelo, MS 38801
601/842-5621 (515)

Small Business Development Center
University of Mississippi
Suite 216, Old Chemistry Bldg
University, MS 38677
601/234-2120   Fax: 601/232-5650

Small Business Development Center
Hinds Community College
1624 Highway 27
Vicksburg, MS 39180
601/638-0600   Fax: 601/857-3474

MISSOURI

Small Business Development Center
University of Missouri
300 University Place
Columbia, MO 65211
314/882-0344   Fax: 314/884-4297

Small Business Development Center
Southeast Missouri State University
222 North Pacific
Cape Girardeau, MO 63701
314/290-5965   Fax: 314/651-5005

Small Business Development Center
University of Missouri-Columbia
1800 University Place
Columbia, MO 65211
314/882-7096   Fax: 314/882-6156

Small Business Development Center
Mineral Area College
P O Box 1000
Flat River, MO 63601
314/431-4593 (283)   Fax: 314/431-6807

Business & Industrial Specialists
University Extension
2507 Industrial Drive
Jefferson City, MO 65101
314/634-2824

Small Business Development Center
DED-Missouri Product Finder
301 West High Room 770
Jefferson City, MO 65102
314/751-4892   Fax: 314/751-8394

Small Business Development Center
Missouri Southern State College
3950 Newman Rd, #107 Matthews Hall
Joplin, MO 64801-1595
417/625-9313   Fax: 816/926-4588

SBDC Rockhurst College
1100 Rockhurst Road
Kansas City, MO 64110-2599
816/926-4572   Fax: 816/926-4588

Small Business Development Center
Northeast Missouri State University
207 East Patterson
Kirksville, MO 63501
816/785-4307   Fax: 816/785-4181

SBDC Northwest Missouri State University
127 South Buchanan
Maryville, MO 64468
816/562-1701   Fax: 816/562-1900

SBDC Three Rivers Community College
Business Incubator Bldg
3019 Fair Street
Poplar Bluff, MO 63901
314/686-3499   Fax: 314/686-5467

SBDC University of Missouri-Rolla
223 Engineering Management Bldg
Rolla, MO 65401-0249
314/341-4561   Fax: 314/341-2071

Center for Tech. Transportation & Economic Development
University of Missouri - Rolla
Room 104, Bldg 1, Nagogami Terrace
Rolla, MO 65401-0249
314/341-4559   Fax: 314/341-4992

SBDC Missouri Western State College
4525 Downs Drive, Student Union 108
St Joseph, MO 64507
816/271-4364

Small Business Development Center
Saint Louis University
3750 Lindell Blvd
St Louis, MO 63108
314/534-7232   Fax: 314/836-6337

SBDC Center for Business Research
SW Missouri State University
Box 88, 901 South National
Springfield, MO 65804-0089
417/836-5685   Fax: 417/836-6337

Small Business Development Center
Central Missouri State University
Grinstead # 75
Warrensburg, MO 64093-5037
816/543-4402   Fax: 816/747-1653

Center for Technology
Central Missouri State University
Grinstead # 75
Warrensburg, MO 64093-5037
816/543-4402   Fax: 816/747-1653

MONTANA

Helena SBDC
Montana Department of Commerce
1424 Ninth Ave
Helena, MT 59620
406/444-4780   Fax: 406/444-2808

Small Business Development Center
Billings Area Business Incubator
115 N Broadway, 2nd Floor
Billings, MT 59101
406/256-6875   Fax: 406/255-7175

Bozeman SBDC
321 East Main, Suite 413
Bozeman, MT 59715
406/587-3113   Fax: 406/587-9565

Butte SBDC - REDI
305 West Mercury, Suie 211
Butte, MT 59701
406/782-7333   Fax: 406/782-9675

Havre SBDC/Bear Paw Development Corp
P O Box 1549
Havre, MT 59501
406/265-9226   Fax: 406/265-3777

SBDC Flathead Valley Community College
777 Grandview Drive
Kalispell, MT 59901
406/756-8333   Fax: 406/756-3815

SBDC Missoula Business Incubator
127 N Higgins, 3rd Floor
Missoula, MT 59802
406/728-9234   Fax: 406/721-4584

Sidney Small Business Development Center
123 West Main
Sidney, MT 59270
406/482-5024   Fax: 406/482-5306

NEBRASKA

NBDC - University of Nebraska at Omaha
60th & DodgeStreet
CBA, Room 407
Omaha, NE 68182
402/554-2521   FAX: 402/554-3747

NBDC Chadron State College
Administration Building
Chadron, NE 69337
308/432-6282

NBDC University of Nebraska at Kearney
Welch Hall, 19th & College Drive
Kearney, NE 68849
308/234-8344

NBDC University of Nebraska at Lincoln
Cornhusker Bank Bldg
11th & Cornhusker Hwy
Lincoln, NE 68521
402/472-3358

NBDC Mid Plains Community College
416 N Jeffers, Room 26
North Platte, NE 69101
308/534-5115

NBDC University of Nebraska at Omaha
Peter Kiewit Conference Center
1313 Farnam-on-the-Mall, Suite 132
Omaha, NE 68182-0248
402/595-2381

NBDC Peru State College
T.J. Majors Hall, Room 248
Peru, NE 68421
402/872-2274

NBDC Scottsbluff
Nebraska Public Power Bldg.
1721 Broadway, Room 408
Scottsbluff, NE 69361
308/635-7513

NBDC Wayne State College
Connell Hall
Wayne, NE 68787
402/375-7575

NEVADA

SBDC University of Nevada-Reno
College of Business Administration, Room 411
Reno, NV 89557-0100
702/784-1717   Fax: 702/784-4337

Small Business Development Center
Northern Nevada Community College
901 Elm Street
Elko, NV 89801
702/738-8493

Small Business Development Center
University of Nevada at Las Vegas
College of Business & Economics
4505 Maryland Pkwy
Las Vegas, NV 89154
702/739-0852

NEW HAMPSHIRE

University of New Hampshire SBDC
108 McConnell Hall
Durham, NH 03824
603/862-2200   Fax: 603/862-4468

SBDC Kingham Farm
University of New Hampshire
Durham, NH 03824
603/743-3995   Fax: 603/743-3997

SBDC University of New Hampshire
108 McConnell Hall
Durham, NH 03824
603/862-2200   Fax: 603/862-4468

Small Business Development Center
Keene State College
Black House
Keene, NH 03431
603/358-2602   Fax: 603/756-4878

Small Business Development Center
P O Box 786
Littleton, NH 03561
603/444-1053

Small Business Development Center
1001 Elm Street
Manchester, NH 03101
603/624-2000   Fax: 603/623-3972

Greater Nashua Chamber of Commerce
188 Main Street, 2nd Floor
Nashua, NH 03060-2731
603/891-2471   Fax: 603/891-2474

SBDC Plymouth State College
Hyde Hall
Plymouth, NH 03264
603/535-2523   Fax: 603/535-2526

NEW JERSEY

SBDC Rutgers University
180 University Ave.
3rd Floor, Ackerson Hall
Newark, NJ 07102
201/648-5950   Fax: 201/648-1110

SBDC / Chamber of Commerce
1301 Atlantic Ave
Atlantic City NJ 08401
609/345-5600

SBDC Rutgers
The State University of Camden-NJ Campus
Business & Science Bldg, 2nd Floor
Point & Pearl Streets
Camden, NJ 08102
609/757-6221

Brookdale Community College SBDC
Newman Springs Road
Lincroft, NJ 07738
201/842-1900 (751)

SBDC Rutgers University at Newark
3rd Floor, Ackerson Hall
180 University Ave
Newark, NJ 07102
201/648-5950

SBDC Mercer County Community College
1200 Old Trenton Road
Trenton, NJ 08690
609/586-4800

Small Business Development Center
Kean College
Morris Ave & Conant
Union, NJ 07083
201/527-2413

SBDC Warren County Community College
Route 57 West   Rd #1 Box 55A
Washington NJ 07882
201/689-7613

NEW MEXICO

NM SBDC Lead Center
Santa Fe Community College
P O Box 4187
Sante Fe, NM 87502-4187
505/438-1362   Fax: 505/438-1237

Small Business Development Center
NM State University Alamogordo
1000 Madison
Alamogordo, NM 88310
505/434-5272

SBDC Albuquerque Tech-Voc Institute
525 Buena Vista SE
Albuquerque, NM 87106
505/224-4246

SBDC NM State University at Carlsbad
P O Box 1090
Carlsbad, NM 88220
505/887-6562

SBDC Clovis Community College
417 Schepps Blvd
Clovis, NM 88101-8345
505/769-4136

SBDC Northern NM Community College
1002 N Onate Street
Espanola, NM 87532
505/753-7141 (248)

SBDC San Juan College
203 W Main Street, Suite 201
Farmington, NM 87401
505/326-4321

SBDC University of New Mexico-Gallup
P O Box 1395
Gallup, NM 87305
505/722-2220

SBDC NM State University at Grants
709 E Roosevelt Ave
Grants, NM 87020
505/287-8221

SBDC New Mexico Junior College
5317 Lovington Hwy
Hobbs, NM 88240
505/392-4510

SBDC NM State Univ. / Dona Ana Branch
Box 30001 Dept 3DA
Las Cruces, NM 88003-0001
505/527-7601

SBDC Luna Vocational-Technical Institute
P O Darwer K
Las Vegas, NM 87701
505/454-2595

Univ. of New Mexico at Los Alamos SBDC
P O Box 715
Los Alamos, NM 87544
505/662-0001

SBDC University of NM at Valencia
280 La Entrada
Los Lunas, NM 87031
505/865-9596 (317)

SBDC Eastern NM Univ at Roswell
P O Box 6000
Roswell, NM 88201-6000
505/624-7133

SBDC Sante Fe Community College
P O Box 4187
Sante Fe, NM 87502-4187
505/438-1343

SBDC Western New Mexico University
P O Box 2672
Silver City, NM 88062
505/538-6320

SBDC Tucumcari Area Vocational School
P O Box 1143
Tucumcari, NM 88401
505/461-4413

NEW YORK

SBDC State University of New York
SUNY Central Plaza S-523
Albany, NY 12246
518/443-5398   Fax: 518/465-4992

SBDC - SUNY at Albany
Draper Hall 107
135 Western Ave
Albany, NY 12222
518/442-5577

SBDC - SUNY at Binghamton
P O Box 6000, Vestal Parkway East
Binghamton, NY 13902-6000
607/777-4024

SBDC Long Island University
Humanities Bldg., 7th Floor
One University Plaza
Brooklyn, NY 11201
718/852-1197

SBDC State University College at Buffalo
BA 117, 1300 Elmwood Ave
Buffalo, NY 14222
716/878-4030

Small Business Development Center
24-28 Denison Parkway West
Corning, NY 14830
607/962-9461

SBDC State University College of Technology
Laffin Administration Bldg., Room 007
Farmingdale, NY 11735
516/420-2765

SBDC York College
Science Bldg., Room107
The City University of New York
Jamaica, NY 11451
718/262-2880

SBDC Jamestown Community College
P O Box 20
Jameston, NY 14702-0020
716/665-5220

SBDC Pace University - Pace Plaza
New York, NY 10038
212/346-1899

SBDC Clinton Community College
Alpert Bldg., Rt 9
Plattsburgh, NY 12901
518/564-7232

SBDC Manhattan College
Farrell Hall
Riverdale, NY 10471
212/884-1880

SBDC Monroe Community College
1000 East Henrietta Road
Rochester, NY 14623
716/292-2000 (3030)

Small Business Development Center
Niagara County Community College
3111 Saunders Settlement Road
Sanborn, NY 14132
716/693-1910

Small Business Development Center
State University at Stony Brook
Harriman Hall, Room 109
Stony Brook, NY 11794
516/632-9070

Small Business Development Center
Ulster County Community College
Stone Ridge, NY 12484
914/687-5272

Small Business Development Center
Rockland Community College
145 College Road
Suffern, NY 10901
914/356-0370

SBDC Greater Syracuse Incubator Center
1201 East Fayette Street
Syracuse, NY 13210
315/475-0083

Small Business Development Center
SUNY Institute of Tech Utica/Rome
P O Box 3050
Utica, NY 13504-3050
315/792-7546

Small Business Development Center
Jefferson Community College
Watertown, NY 13601
315/782-9262

NORTH CAROLINA

NC SBDC Headquarters Office
University of NC at Chapel Hill
4509 Creedmoor Road, Suite 201
Raleigh, NC 27612
919/571-4154   Fax: 919/787-9284

Northwestern Regional Center
Appalachian State University
Walker College of Business
Boone, NC 28608
704/262-2095

Southern Piedmont Regional Center
Univ of N. Carolina at Charlotte
Ben Craig Center
8701 Mallard Creek Road
Charlotte, NC 28262
704/548-1090

Western Regional Center
Western Carolina University
Center for Improving Mountain Living
Cullowhee, NC 28723
704/227-7494

NE Regional Center
Elizabeth City State University
Weeksville Road, P O Box 874
K.E. White Graduate Center
Elizabeth City, NC 27909
919/335-3247

Cape Fear Area Center
Fayetteville State University
P O Box 1334
Fayetteville, NC 28302
919/486-1727

E. Regional Center / E. Carolina University
Corner First & Reade Streets
Greeneville, NC 27858-4353
919/757-6157

N. Piedmont Regional Center-Eastern Office
University of NC at Greensboro
P O Box D-22
Greensboro, NC 27411
919/334-7005

Research Triangle Park Regional Center
University of North Carolina at Chapel Hill
4509 Creedmoor Road, Suite 201
Raleigh, NC 27612
919/571-4154

Southeastern Regional Center
University of North Carolina at Wilmington
Room 131, Cameron Hall
Wilmington, NC 28403
919/395-3744

Northern Piedmont Regional Center
Winston-Salem State University
PO Box 13025
Winston-Salem, NC 27110
919/750-2030

NORTH DAKOTA

State Center / Grand Forks
118 Gamble Hall, UND, Box 7308
Grand Forks, ND 58202-7308
701/777-3700   Fax: 701/777-5099

Bismark Regional Center SBDC
400 E Broadway, Suite 421
Bismark, ND 58501
701/223-8583   Fax: 701/222-3843

Dickinson Regional Center SBDC
314 3rd Ave West, Drawer L
Dickinson, ND 58602
701/227-2096   Fax: 701/225-5116

Grand Forks Reg Center SBDC
Hemmp Center
1407 24th Ave S, Suite 201
Grand Forks, ND 58201
701/772-8502   Fax: 701/775-2772

Fargo Regional Center
Small Business Development Center
417 Main Street
Fargo, ND 58103
701/237-0986   Fax: 701/235-6706

Minot Regional Center
Small Business Development Center
1020 20th Ave SW
Minot, ND 58702
701/852-8861   Fax: 701/838-2488

OHIO

Small Business Development Center
77 South High Street
Columbus, OH 43226
614/466-2711   Fax: 614/466-0829

SBDC Women's Entrepreneurial Center
400 Elbon Ave
Akron, OH 43309
216/773-0436

SBDC Akron Regional Development Board
8th Floor, One Cascade Plaza
Akron, OH 44308
216/379-3170

SBDC Northwest Technical College
Box 245-A, Route 1
Archbold, OH 43502
419/267-3331

SBDC Ohio Hi-Point JVC
2280 State Route 540
Bellefontaine, OH 43311
513/559-3010

SBDC Stark Develoment Board
800 Savannah Ave NE
Canton, OH 44704
216/453-5900

SBDC - City of Cambridge
1131 Steubenville Ave
Cambridge, OH 43725
614/439-2822

Small Business Development Center
Wright State Branch Campus
7600 State Route 703
Celina, OH 45822
419/586-2365

SBDC University of Cincinnati
IAMS Research Park
1111 Edison Drive, Mail Loc #189
Cincinnati, OH 45216
513/948-2082

SBDC Council of Smaller Enterprises
200 Tower City Center
Cleveland, OH 44113
216/621-3300

Small Business Development Center
37 North High Street
Columbus, OH 43216
614/221-1321

Small Business Development Center
Chamber Plaza: 5th & Main Street
Dayton, OH 45402
513/226-8213

Small Business Development Center
Terra Technical College
1220 Cedar Street
Freemont, OH 43420
419/334-3886

Small Business Development Center
Southern State Community College
100 Hobart Drive
Hillsboro, OH 45133
513/393-3431

Small Business Development Center
36 West Walnut Street
Jefferson, OH 44047
216/576-9126

Small Business Development Center
Lima Technical College
545 West Market Street, Suite 305
Lima, OH 45801
419/229-5320

SBDC Greater Lorain
Chamber of Commerce
204 Fifth Street
Lorain, OH 44052
216/244-2292

SBDC - Mid-Ohio
P O Box 1208
Mansfield, OH 44901
419/525-1614

SBDC Miami University DSC Dept
311 Upham Hall
Oxford, OH 45056
513/529-4841

Small Business Development Center
Upper Valley Joint Vocational School
8811 Career Drive
Piqua, OH 4535
513/778-8419

SBDC / Dept of Devopment of CIC
100 East Main Street
St Clairsville, OH 43950
614/695-9678

Small Business Development Center
Sandusky City Schools
407 Decatur Street
Sandusky, OH 44870
419/626-6940

SBDC Lawrence County Chamber of Comm.
US Route 52 & Solida Road
Southpoint, OH 45680
614/894-3838

SBDC / Chamber of Commerce
P O Box 278
Steubenville, OH 43952
614/282-6226

Small Business Development Center
Enterprise Bldg Suite 200
300 Madison Ave
Toledo, OH 43604-1575
419/243-8191

Small Business Development Center
Youngstown State University
Cushwa Center for Industrial Development
Youngstown, OH 44555
216/742-3495

SBDC Zanesville Area Chamber
217 North Fifth Street
Zanesville, OH 43701
614/452-4868

OKLAHOMA

SBDC - SE Oklahoma State University
Station A, Box 2584
Durant, OK 74701
405/924-0277   Fax: 405/924-7071

SBDC - East Central University
1036 East 10th
Ada, OK 74820
405/436-3190

Northwestern State University SBDC
Alva, OK 73717
405/327-5883

SBDC - Southeastern State University
517 University Blvd
Durant, OK 74701
405/924-0277

SBDC - Central State University
100 North University Blvd
Edmond, OK 73034
405/359-1968

Enid Satellite Center - SBDC
Phillips Univ - 100 S University Ave
Enid, OK 73701
405/242-7989

SBDC - Langston University Center
P O Box 667
Langston, OK 73050
405/466-3924

Lawton Satellite Center - SBDC
601 SW "D", Suite 209
Lawton, OK 73501
405/248-4946

International Trade Office / Rose State College
6420 Southeast 15th
Midwest City, OK 73110
405/736-0328

Procurement Specialty Ctr/Rose St. College
6420 Southeast 15th
Midwest City, OK 73110
405/733-7348

SBDC Oklahoma Department of Commerce
6601 Broadway Extension
Oklahoma City, OK 73116
1-800-999-6652

Poteau Satellite Center
SBDC Carl Albert Junior College
1507 South McKenna
Poteau, OK 74953
918/647-4019

NE Oklahoma State University SBDC
Tahlequah, OK 74464
918/458-0802

Tulsa Satellite Center SBDC
100 Petroleum Club Bldg
601 S Boulder
Tulsa, OK 74119
918/587-8324

SBDC - SW Oklahoma State University
100 Campus Drive
Weatherford, OK 73096
405/774-1040

OREGON

SBDC Lane Community College
99 W 10th Ave, Suite 216
Eugene, OR 97401
503/726-2250   Fax: 503/345-6006

SBDC Linn-Benton Community College
6500 SW Pacific Blvd
Albany, OR 97321
503/967-6112   Fax: 503/967-6550

SBDC Southern Oregon State College
Regional Services Institute
Ashland, OR 97520
503/482-5838   Fax: 503/482-1115

SBDC Central Oregon Community College
2600 NW College Way
Bend, OR 97701
503/385-5524   Fax: 503/385-5497
1-800-422-3041 (524)

SBDC SW Oregon Community College
340 Central
Coos Bay, OR 97420
503/267-2300   Fax: 503/269-0323

SBDC Columbia Gorge Community College
212 Washington
The Dalles, OR 97058
503/296-1173   Fax: 503/296-2107

SBDC Lane Community College
1059 Willamette Street
Eugene, OR 97401
503/726-2255   Fax: 503/686-0096

SBDC Rogue Community College
290 NE "C" Street
Grants Pass, OR 97526
503/471-3515

SBDC Mount Hood Community College
323 NE Roberts Street
Gresham, OR 97030
503/667-7658   Fax: 503/666-1140

SBDC Oregon Institute of Technology
3201 Campus Drive South 314
Klamath Falls, OR 97601
503/885-1760   Fax: 503/885-1115

SBDC Oregon Coast Community College
4157 NW Highway 101 Suite 123
Lincoln City, OR 97367
503/994-4166   Fax: 503/996-4958

Southern Oregon St College/Medford SBDC
Regional Services Institute
229 N Barlett
Medford, OR 97501
503/772-3478   Fax: 503/776-2224

SBDC Clackamas Community College
7616 SE Harmony Road
Milwaukee, OR 97222
503/656-4447   Fax: 503/652-0389

SBDC Treasure Valley Community College
88 SW Third Ave
Ontario, OR 97914
503/889-2617   Fax: 503/889-8331

SBDC Blue Mountain Community College
37 SE Dorion
Pendleton, OR 97801
503/276-6233

SBDC Portland Community College
123 NW Second Ave, Suite 321
Portland, OR 97209
503/273-2828   Fax: 503/294-0725

SBDC International Trade Program
121 SW Salmon Street, Suite 210
Portland, OR 97204
503/274-7482   Fax: 503/228-6350

Small Business Development Center
Umpqua Community College
744 SE Rose
Roseburg, OR 97470
503/672-2535   Fax: 503/672-3679

Small Business Development Center
Chemeketa Community College
365 Ferry Street SE
Salem, OR 97301
503/399-5181   Fax: 503/581-6017

SBDC Clatstop Community College
1240 South Holladay
Seaside, OR 97138
503/738-3347   Fax: 503/738-3347
(call before faxing)

SBDC Tillamook Bay Community College
401 B Main Street
Tillamook, OR 97141
503/842-2551   Fax: 503/842-2555

PENNSYLVANIA

SBDC University of Pennsylvania
The WhartonSchool 444 Vance Hall
Philadelphia, PA 19104
215/898-1219   Fax: 215/573-2135

SBDC Lehigh University
Rauch Business Center #37
Bethlehem, PA 18015
215/758-3980

Small Business Development Center
Clarion University of Pennsylvania
Dana Still Bldg
Clarion, PA 16214
814/226-2060

SBDC Gannon University
Carlisle Bldg., 3rd Floor
Erie, PA 16541
814/871-7714

SBDC Kutztown University
2986 N 2nd Street
Harrisburg, PA 17110
717/233-3120

SBDC St Vincent College
Alfred Hall 4th Floor
Latrobe, PA 15650
412/537-4572

Bucknell University SBDC
Dana Engineering Bldg 1st Floor
Lewisburg, PA 17837
717/524-1249

SBDC St Francis College
Business Resource Center
Loretto, PA 15940
814/472-3200

Small Business Development Center
PA State Univ., The Capital College
Crags Building - Route 230
Middleton, PA 17057
717/233-3120

Small Business Development Center
LaSalle University
20th and Olney Ave
Philadelphia, PA 19141
215/951-1416

Small Business Development Center
Temple University
Room 6 Speakman Hall 006-00
Philadelphia, PA 19122
215/787-7282

Small Business Development Center
University of Pennsylvania
The Wharton School, 409 Vance Hall
Phildelphia, PA 19104
215/898-4861

Small Business Development Center
University of Pittsburgh
Room 343 Mervis Hall
Pittsburgh, PA 15260
412/648-1544

SBDC Duquesne University
Rockwell Hall, Room 10 Concourse
600 Forbes Ave
Pittsburgh, PA 15282
412/434-6233

Small Business Development Center
University of Scranton
St Thomas Hall, Room 588
Scranton, PA 18503
717/941-7588

SBDC Wilkes University
192 South Franklin Street
Wilkes-Barr, PA 18766
717/824-4651 (4340)

PUERTO RICO

SBDC University of Puerto Rico
P O Box 5253, College Station
Mayaguez, PR 00681
809/834-3590   Fax: 809/834-3790

Small Business Development Center
Interamerican University / Casa Llompart
P O Box 1293
Hato Rey, PR 00917
809/765-2335

Small Business Development Center
University of Puerto Rico at Humacao
Box 10226, CUH Station
Humacao, PR 00661
809/850-2500

SBDC Univ. of Puerto Rico at Mayaguez
P O Box 5253 College Station
Mayaguez, PR 00681
809/834-3590

SBDC University of PR at Ponce
P O Box 7186
Ponce, PR 00732
809/841-2641

Small Business Development Center
University of Peurto Rico at Rio Piedras
P O Box 21417, UPR Station
Rio Piedras, PR 00931
809/763-5933

RHODE ISLAND

Bryant College RISBDC - State Office
1150 Douglas Pike
Smithfield, RI 02917
401/232-6111   Fax: 401/232-6416

RISBDC University of Rhode Island
24 Woodward Hall
Kingston, RI 02881
401/792-2451   Fax: 401/792-4017

Aquidneck Island RISBDC
28 Jacome Way
Middletown, RI 02840
401/849-6900   Fax: 401/849-0815

Bryant College RISBDC
Downtown Providence Office
7 Jackson Walkway
Providence, RI 02903
401/831-1330   Fax: 401/454-2819

RISBDC Community College of RI
Providence Campus, One Hilton St
Providence, RI 02905
401/455-6042   Fax: 401/455-6047

Bryant College RISBDC
1150 Douglas Pike
Smithfield, RI 02917
401/232-6115

SOUTH CAROLINA

Small Business Development Center
University of South Carolina
1710 College Street
Columia, SC 29208
803/777-4907   Fax: 803/777-4403

Lowcountry SBDC
University of South Carolina - Beaufort
800 Carteret Street
Beaufort, SC 29902
803/524-7112 (4143)

Small Business Development Center
P O Box 20339
Charleston, SC 29413-0339
803/727-2020

Small Business Development Center
Clemson University
College of Commerce & Industry
425 Sirrine Hall
Clemson, SC 29634
803/656-3227

Small Business Development Center
University of South Carolina
College of Business Administration
Columbia, SC 29208
803/777-5118

Small Business Development Center
Coastal Carolina College
School of Business Administration
Conway, SC 29526
803/349-2169

SBDC Greenville Technical College
Box 5616 Station S, Administarion Annex
Greenville, SC 29606
803/271-4259

Small Business Development Center
Florence Darlington Technical College
P O Box 100548
Florence, SC 29501
803/661-8256

Upper Savannah Council of Government
P O Box 1366
Greenwood, SC 29648
803/227-6110

Small Business Development Center
University of South Carolina - Augusta
Triangle Plaza Hwy 25
North Augusta, SC 29841
803/442-3670

Small Business Development Center
South Carolina State College
School of Business
Orangeburg, SC 29117
803/536-8445

Small Business Development Center
Winthrop College, School of Bus. Admin.
119 Thurmond Bldg
Rock Hill, SC 29733
803/323-2283   Fax: 803/323-3960

Small Business Development Center
Spartanburg Technical College
PO Box 1636
Nations Plaza Headquarters
Spartanburg, SC 29305
803/591-3726

SOUTH DAKOTA

Small Business Development Center
University of South Dakota
414 East Clark
Vermillion, SD 57069
605/677-5272   Fax: 605/677-5427

Small Business Development Center
226 Citizens Bldg
Aberdeen, SD 57401
605/225-2252

Small Business Development Center
105 South Euclid, Suite C
Pierre, SD 57501
605/773-5941

Small Business Development Center
444 Mount Rushmore Road, #208
Rapid City, SD 57709
605/394-5311

Small Business Development Center
200 North Phillips, L103
Sioux Falls, SD 57102
605/339-3366

SBDC University of South Dakota
414 East Clark
Vermillion, SD 57069
605/677-5279

TENNESSEE

SBDC - Memphis State University
Bldg 1, South Campus
Memphis, TN 38152
901/678-2500   Fax: 901/678-4072

Business Dev. Cntr./SE Tenn. Dev. District
100 Cherokee Blvd
Chattanooga, TN 37405
615/752-4308

SBDC Austin Peay State University
College of Business
Clarksville, TN 37044
615/648-7674

SBDC Cleveland State Community College
Adkisson Drive, PO Box 3570
Cleveland, TN 37320
615/478-6247

SBDC Tennessee Technical University
College of Business Administration
P O Box 5023
Cookeville, TN 38505
615/372-3648

Small Business Development Center
Dyersburg State Community College
Office Extension Service, PO Box 648
Dyersburg, TN 38024
901/286-3267

SBDC Jackson State Community College
2046 North Parkway Street
Jackson, TN 38305
901/424-5389

Small Business Development Center
East Tennessee State University
College of Business
Johnson City, TN 37614
615/929-5630

Small Business Development Center
Pellissippi State Technical Commission
3435 Division Street
Knoxville, TN 37933
615/694-6661

Small Business Development Center
Memphis State University
320 S Dudley St
Memphis, TN 38104
901/527-1041

SBDC Walters State Community College
500 S Davy Crockett Pkwy
Morrisontown, TN 37813
615/587-9722 (447)

SBDC Middle Tennessee State University
School of Business
1417 East Main Street
Murfreesboro, TN 37132
615/898-2745

Small Business Development Center
TN State University - School of Business
330 10th Ave North
Nashville, TN 37203
615/251-1178

TEXAS

North Texas - Dallas SBDC
Bill J Priest Inst. for Econonic Development
1402 Corinth St
Dallas, TX 75215
214/565-5833   Fax: 214/565-5815

Small Business Development Center
Trinity Valley Community College
500 South Prairieville
Athens, TX 75751
903/675-6230

Small Business Development Center
Sam Rayburn Library
Bonham, TX 75148
214/583-7025

Small Business Development Center
120 North 12th Street
Corsicana, TX 75110
903/874-0658

Small Business Development Center
Center for Gov't Contracting
1402 Corinth
Dallas, TX 75215
214/565-5842   Fax: 214/565-5857

International SBDC
2050 Stemmons Frwy, Suite #150
World Trade Center, PO Box 58299
Dallas, TX 75258
214/653-1777   Fax: 214/748-5774

Small Business Development Center
Dallas County Community College
1402 Corinth
Dallas, TX 75215
214/565-5836   Fax: 214/565-5857

Small Business Development Center
Grayson Community College
6101 Grayson Dr
Denison, TX 75020
903/463-8654   Fax: 214/463-5284

Small Business Development Center
P O Box P
Denton, TX 76201
817/382-7151   Fax: 817/382-0040

Small Business Development Center
214 South Main, Suite 101 D
Duncanville, TX 75116
214/709-5878

Small Business Development Center
Tarrant County Junior College
1500 Houston, Suite 163
Ft Worth, TX 76102
817/877-9254

Small Business Development Center
1525 West California
Gainesville, TX 76240
817/665-4785   Fax: 817/668-6049

Small Business Development Center
SOS Building
P O Box 619
Hillsboro, TX 76645
817/582-2555 (382)

Small Business Development Center
Kilgore College
300 South High
Longview, TX 75601
903/763-2642

Small Business Development Center
NE Texas Community College
P O Box 1307
Mt Pleasant, TX 75455
903/572-1911   Fax: 903/572-6712

SBDC Paris Jr College
2400 Clarksville
St Paris, TX 75460
903/784-1802

SBDC Collin County Community College
Plano Market Square
1717 E Spring Creek Pkwy, #109
Plano, TX 75074
214/881-0506

SBDC Tyler Jr College
1530 South SW Loop 323, Suite 100
Tyler, TX 75701
903/510-2975   Fax: 903/510-2978

SBDC McLennan Community College
4601 North 19th Street
Waco, TX 76708
817/750-3600   Fax: 817/756-0776

Small Business Development Center
University of Houston
601 Jefferson, Suite 2330
Houston, TX 77002
713/752-8444   Fax: 713/752-8484

SBDC Alvin Community College
3110 Mustang Rd
Alvin TX 77511-4898
713/388-4686

Small Business Development Center
Lee College
Rundell Hall
511South Whiting Street
Baytown, TX 77520-4796
713/425-6309   Fax: 713/425-6307

SBDC John Gray Institute/Lamar Univ.
855 Florida Ave
Beaumont, TX 77705
409/880-2367   Fax: 409/880-2201
1-800-722-3443

Small Business Development Center
Blinn College, 902 College Ave
Brenham, TX 77833
409/830-4137   Fax: 409/830-4116

Small Business Development Center
Galveston College
4015 Avenue Q
Galveston, TX 77550
409/740-7380   Fax: 409/740-7381

SBDC Houston Lead Center
601 Jefferson, Suite 2330
Houston, TX 77002
713/752-8400   Fax: 713/752-8484

Texas Info Procurement Service SBDC
1100 Louisianna, Suite #500
Houston, TX 77002
713/752-8477   Fax: 713/752-8484

International Trade Center
601 Jefferson, Suite 2330
Houston, TX 77002
713/752-8404

Small Business Development Center
Sam Houston State University
College of Bus Admin., P O Box 2056
Huntsville, TX 77341
409/294-3737   Fax: 409/294-3612

SBDC N Harris County College
Administration Bldg, Room 104
20000 Kingwood Drive
Kingwood, TX 77339
713/359-1677   Fax: 713/359-1612

SBDC Brazosport College
500 College Dr
Lake Jackson, TX 77566
409/265-7208   Fax: 409/265-2944

SBDC Angelina College
P O Box 1768
Lufkin, TX 75902-1768
409/639-1887   Fax: 409/634-8726

Houston Community College SBDC
13600 Murphy Road
Stafford, TX 77477
713/499-4870   Fax: 713/499-8194

Small Business Development Center
College of the Mainland
8419 Emmett F. Lowry Expressway
Texas City, TX 77591
713/499-4870   Fax: 713/499-8194

Small Business Development Center
Wharton County Jr College
Administration Bldg, Room 102
911 Boling Hwy
Wharton, TX 77488-0080
409/532-4560 (246)   Fax: 409/532-2201

NW Texas SBDC
Center for Innovation
2579 South Loop 289, Suite 114
Lubbock, TX 79423
806/745-3973   Fax: 806/745-6207

Abilene Christian University SBDC
ACU Station Box 8307
Abilene, TX 79699
915/674-2776   Fax: 915/674-2507

Panhandle Small Business Development Ctr
1800 S Washignton, Suite 110
Amarillo, TX 79102
806/372-5151   Fax: 806/372-3939

Texas Tech University
Small Business Development Center
Center for Innovation
2579 South Loop 289, Suite 114
Lubbock, TX 79423
806/745-1637   Fax: 806/745-6207

Small Business Development Center
4901 E University
Odessa, TX 79762
915/563-0400   Fax: 915/561-5534

Small Business Development Center
Tarleton St. University - College of Business
Box T-158
Stephenville, TX 76402
817/968-9330   Fax: 817/968-9329

Midwestern State University SBDC
3400 Taft Blvd
Witchita Falls, TX 76308
817/696-6738   Fax: 817/696-8303

Small Business Development Center
UTSA Downtown Center
801 S Bowie Street
San Antonio, TX 78205
512/224-0791   Fax: 512/222-9834

Austin Small Business Development Center
2211 Soth IH 35, Suite 103
Austin, TX 78741
512/326-2256   Fax: 512/447-9825

Corpus Christi Chamber of Commerce
Small Business Development Center
1201 North Shoreline
Corpus Christi, TX 78403
512/882-6161   Fax: 512/888-5627

University of Texas - Pan American
Small Business Development Center
1201 West University
Edinburg, TX 78539-2999
512/381-3361   Fax: 512/381-2322

Small Business Development Center
El Paso Community College
103 Montana Ave, Suite 202
El Paso, TX 79902-3929
915/534-3410   Fax: 915/534-3420

Kingsville Chamber of Commerce SBDC
635 E King
Kingsville, TX 78363
512/595-5088   Fax: 512/592-0866

Laredo Development Foundation SBDC
616 Leal Street
Laredo, TX 78041
512/722-0563   Fax: 512/722-6247

Small Business Development Center
Angelo State University
2601 West Ave N, Campus Box 10910
San Angelo, TX 76909
915/942-2098   Fax: 915/942-2038

UTSA Small Business Development Center
801 S Bowie Street
San Antonio, TX 78205
512/224-0791   Fax: 512/222-9834

UTSA International SBDC
801 S Bowie Street
San Antonio, TX 78205
512/227-2997   Fax: 512/222-9834

Middle Rio Grande Devel. Council SBDC
209 North Getty Street
Uvalde, TX 78801
512/278-2527   Fax: 512/278-2929

University of Houston-Victoria SBDC
700 Main Center, Suite 102
Victoria, TX 77901
512/575-8944   Fax: 512/575-8852

UTAH

SBDC University of Utah
102 West 500 South, Suite 315
Salt Lake City, UT 84101
801/581-7905   Fax: 801/581-7814

Small Business Development Center
Southern Utah University
351 West Center
Cedar City, UT 84720
801/586-5401   Fax: 801/586-5493

Small Business Development Center
Snow College
465 West 1st North
Ephraim, UT 84627
801/283-4021   Fax: 801/283-6879

Small Business Development Center
Utah State Univ - East Campus Bldg
Logan, UT 84322-8330
801/750-2277   Fax: 801/750-3749

SBDC Weber State University
School of Business & Economics
Ogden, UT 84408-3806
801/626-7323   Fax: 801/626-7423

SBDC College of Eastern Utah
451 East 400 North
Price, UT 84501
801/637-1995   Fax: 801/637-4102

SBDC Dixie College
225 South 700 East
St George, UT 84770
801/673-4811 (455)   Fax: 801/673-8552

VERMONT

Vermont SBDC
PO Box 422
Randolph, VT 05060-0422
802/728-9101 or 800/464-SBDC

Brattleboro Development Credit Corp.
P.O. Box 1177
Brattleboro, VT 05301-1177
802/257-7731

Greater Burlington Industrial Corp.
P.O. Box 786
Burlington, VT 05402-0786
802/862-5726

Addison County Economic Develop. Corp.
2 Court St.
Middlebury, VT   05753
802/388-7953

Central VT Economic Development Corp.
PO Box 1439
Montpelier, VT 05601-1439
802/223-4654

Lamoille Industrial Development Corp.
PO Box 455
Morrisville, VT   05661-0455
802/888-5640

Bennington County Industrial Corp.
PO Box 357
North Bennington, VT 05257-0357
802/442-8975

Lake Champlain Island
Chamber of Commerce
PO Box 213
North Hero, VT 05474-0213
802/372-5683

Rutland Industrial Development Corp.
PO Box 39
Rutland, VT   05701-0039
802/773-9147

Franklin County Industrial Development Corp.
PO Box 1099
St. Albans, VT 05478-1099
802/524-2194

NE Vermont Development Association
PO Box 640
St. Johnsbury, VT 05819-0640
802/748-1014 or 748-5181

Springfield Regional Development Corp.
PO Box 58
Springfield, VT 05156-0058
802/885-2071 or 885-3061

VIRGINIA

Virginia Small Business Development Ctr.
Dept of Economic Development
1021 East Cary St, 11 Floor
Richmond, VA 23219
804/371-8258   Fax: 804/371-8185

Arlington Small Business Development Ctr.
GMU Arlington Campus
3401 N Fairfax Campus
Arlington, VA 22201
703/993-8129   Fax: 703/993-8130

Southwest SBDC
Mt Empire Community College
Drawer 700, Route 23
Big Stone Gap, VA 24219
703/523-6529   Fax: 703/523-4130

Western Virginia
Small Business Development Center
Consortium VPI & SU

Economic Development Assistance Center
404 Clay Street
Blacksburg, VA 24061-0539
703/231-5278   Fax: 703/953-2307

Central Virginia SBDC
918 Emmet St North, #200
Charlottesville, VA 22903-4878
804/295-8198   Fax: 804/979-3749

SBDC Longwood College
Farmville, VA 23901
804/395-2086   Fax: 804/395-2359

Northern Virginia SBDC
4260 Chainbridge Road, Suite B-1
Fairfax, VA 22030
703/993-2131   Fax: 703/993-2126

SBDC James Madison University
College of Business Bldg, Room 523
Harrisonburg, VA 22807
703/568-3227   Fax: 703/568-3299

Lynchburg Region SBDC
147 Mill Ridge Road
Lynchburg, VA 24502
804/582-6100   Fax: 804/582-6106

Small Business Development Center
10311 Sudley Manor Drive
Manassas, VA 22110
703/335-2500   Fax: 703/335-1700

SBDC of Hampton Roads Inc
420 Bank Street
Norlfolk, VA 23501
804/622-6414   Fax: 804/622-5563

Small Business Development Center
New River Valley Planning District Commission Office
1612 Wadsworth Street
Radford, VA 24143
703/731-9546   Fax: 703/831-6093

Southwest SBDC
SW VA Community College
P O Box SVCC
Richlands, VA 24641
703/964-7345   Fax: 703/964-9307

Virginia SBDC
1021 East Cary Street, 11th Floor
Richmond, VA 23219
804/371-8258   Fax: 804/371-8185

Capital Area SBDC
403 East Grace Street
Richmond, VA 23219
804/648-7838   Fax: 804/648-7849

Western VA SBDC Consortium
The Blue Ridge SBDC
310 1st Street, SW Mezzanine
Roanoke, VA 24011
703/983-0717   Fax: 703/983-0723

Longwood SBDC
South Boston Branch
P O Box 1116
South Boston, VA 24592
804/575-0044   Fax: 804/572-4087

Loudoun County SBDC
21515 Ridgetop Circle, Suite 220
Sterling, VA 20166
703/430-7222   Fax: 703/430-9562

Western VA SBDC Consortium
Wytheville Community College
1000 E Main Street
Wytheville, VA 24382
703/228-5541 (314)   Fax: 703/228-2542

VIRGIN ISLANDS

Small Business Development Center
University of the Virgin Islands
United Plaza Shopping Center
Suite 1, Sion Farm
St Croix, VI 00820
809/778-8270

WASHINGTON

Washington State University SBDC
245 Todd Hall
Pullman, WA 99164-4727
509/335-1576   Fax: 509/335-0949

SBDC Bellevue Community College
13555 Bel-Red Road #208
Bellevue, WA 98005
206/643-2888

SBDC West Washington University
415 Park Hall
Bellingham, WA 98225-9073
206/676-3899

SBDC Centralia Community College
600 West Locust Street
Centralia, WA 98531
206/736-9391

SBDC Columbia Basin College
TRIDEC 901 North Colorado
Kennewick, WA 99336
509/735-6222

SBDC Edmonds Community College
20000 68th Ave W.
Lynnwood, WA 98036-5912
206/640-1500

Small Business Development Center
6600 196th Street, SW
Lynnwood WA 98036-5900
206/259-0002

SBDC Big Bend Community College
28th and Chanute
Moses Lake, WA 98837
509/762-6289

Small Business Development Center
Skagit Valley College
2405 College Way
Mt Vernon, WA 98273
206/428-1282

SBDC Washington State University
721 Columbia Street SW
Olympia, WA 98501
206/753-5616

Small Business Development Center
Wenatchee Valley College
P O Box 741
Okanogan, WA 98840-0741
509/826-5107

Business Developement Specialists
DTED Business Assistance Center
919 Lakeridge Way, Suite A
Olympia, WA 98502
206/586-4854

SBDC North Seattle Community College
International Trade Institute
9600 College Way North
Seattle, WA 98103
206/527-3733

Small Business Development Center
2001 6th Ave Suite 2608
Seattle, WA 98121
206/464-5450

Small Business Development Center
Duwamish Industrial Educational Center
6770 East Marginal Way South
Seattle, WA 98108
206/764-5375

Small Business Development Center
WSU-Spokane West 601, 1st Street
Spokane, WA 99204
509/456-2781

Small Business Development Center
950 Pacific Ave, Suite 300
Tacoma, WA 98401
206/272-7232

Small Business Development Center
Columbia River EDC
100 East Columbia Way
Vancouver, WA 98660
206/693-2555

Small Business Development Center
Grand Central Bldg
25 North Wenatchee Ave
Wenatchee, WA 98801
509/662-8016

Small Business Development Center
Yakima Valley College
P O Box 1647
Yakima, WA 98907
509/575-2284

WEST VIRGINIA

Small Business Development Center
Governor's Office of Commerce & Industry
1115 Virginia St - East Captial Complx
Charleston, WV 25301
304/348-2960   Fax: 304/348-0127

Small Business Development Center
Concord College-Center
for Economic Action
Box D-125
Athens, WV 24712
304/384-5103

Small Business Development Center
Bluefield State College
Bluefield, WV 24701
304/327-4107

Small Business Development Center
Governor's Office of Commerce & Industry
1115 Virginia St - East Captial Complx
Charleston, WV 25301
304/348-2960

Small Business Development Center
Fairmont State College
Fairmont, WV 26554
304/367-4125

Small Business Development Center
Marshall University
1050 Fourth Ave
Huntington, WV 25701
304/696-6789

Small Business Development Center
Potomac State College
Keyser, WV 26726
304/788-3011

Small Business Development Center
West Virginia Institute of Technology
Room 102 Engineering Bldg
Montgomery, WV 25136
304/442-5501

Small Business Development Center
West Virginia Univ / P O Box 6025
Morgantown, WV 26506
304/293-5839

Small Business Development Center
West VA University at Parkersburg
Route 5 Box 167-A
Parkersburg, WV 26101
304/424-8277

SBDC Shepherd College
White Hall, Rm101
Shepherdstown, WV 25443
1-800-344-5231 (261)

Small Business Development Center
West Virginia Northern Community College
College Square
Wheeling, WV 26003
304/233-5900

WISCONSIN

Small Business Development Center
University of Wisconsin
432 North Lake Street, Room 423
Madison, WI 53706
608/263-7794   Fax: 608/262-3878

Small Business Development Center
University o f Wisconsin - Eau Claire
Schnieder Hall #113
Eau Claire, WI 54701
715/836-5811

Small Business Development Center
University of Wisconsin at Green Bay
Wood Hall, Suite 460
Green Bay, WI 54311
414/465-2089

Small Business Development Center
University of WI at Parkside
234 Tallent Hall
Kenosha, WI 53141
414/553-2620

Small Business Development Center
University of Wisconsin at La Crosse
323 N Hall
La Crosse, WI 54601
608/785-8782

Small Business Development Center
University of WI at Madison
905 University Ave
Madison, WI 53706
608/263-2221

Small Business Development Center
University of Wisconsin at Milwaukee
929 North Sixth Street
Milwaukee, WI 53203
414/227-3226

SBDC - University of WI at Oshkosh
Clow Faculty Bldg, Room 157
Oshkosh, WI 54901
414/424-1453

Small Business Development Center
University of Wisconsin
Lower Level
Stevens Point, WI 54481
715/346-2004

Small Business Development Center
University of WI at Superior
29 Sundquist Hall
Superior, WI 54880
715/394-8352

Small Business Development Center
University of Wisconsin at Whitewater
2000 Carlson Bldg
Whitewater, WI 53190
414/472-3217

WYOMING

Small Business Development Center
Laramie County Community College
1400 East College Drive
Cheyenne, WY 82007
307/778-1222

Small Business Development Center
Eastern Wyoming College
203 North 6th Street
Douglas, WY 82633
307/358-4090   Fax: 307/358-5629

Small Business Development Center
Northern WY Community College
District - Gillette
720 W 8th Street
Gillette, WY 82716
307/686-0297   Fax: 307/686-0339

Small Business Development Center
Central Wyoming College
360 Main Street
Lander, WY 82520
307/332-3394   or 1-800-735-8394

Small Business Development Center
University of Wyoming
P O Box 3275
Laramie, WY 82071
307/766-2363   Fax: 307/766-4028

Small Business Development Center
Northwest College
146 S Bent Street
Powell, WY 82435
307/754-3746   Fax: 307/754-9368

Small Business Development Center
Western WY Community College
P O Box 428
Rock Springs, WY 82902
307/382-1830   Fax: 307/382-7665

INTERNATIONAL LICENSE NEGOTIATING THESAURUS

The following list of words and phrases is intended to help negotiators in international licensing to more clearly understand each other and to generally improve communications. This is a special list of words and phrases that may have plural or different meanings and includes suggestions on the most appropriate word or phrase or a possible resolution of misunderstandings. This list is not intended to be a dictionary. The list will alert the international negotiator of potential misunderstandings.

This list is taken from the LES Basics of Licensing Book, *and is printed by permission of Licensing Executives Society, 71 East Avenue, Suite S, Norwalk, CT 06851.*

Act of God

An event beyond the reasonable control of the parties preventing the carrying out of an obligation. Words or phrases sometimes used for the same meaning: force majeure, catastrophic event or happening, event not under control of a party. Preferred phrase: force majeure.

Affiliate

See Subsidiary.

Agreement

A binding contract between parties such as a license, however some countries such as China interpret an agreement as non binding but a contract is considered binding. Preferred term: contract or license contract.

Agreement date

See Execution date and Effective date.

Agreement not to license others

See Sole license.

Arms-length transaction

Idiomatic English, means a transaction between strangers who have no financial interest in each other or no ties. May present difficulties in translation.

Assign, assignment

Used primarily in connection with the transfer of the tangible evidence of a right such as a patent or trademark or copyright. Words sometimes used for the same meaning: grant, transfer, convey. Preferred word: assign or assignment. See Exclusive license.

Authorize

See License.

Available to the public

See Generally known to the public and Public domain. Term is not equivalent to "generally known to the public" since something is available to the public in a library may not be generally known.

Best effort

Means the degree of commitment to an obligation. Has been interpreted by some court decisions to mean surprisingly high degrees of effort, perhaps the highest degree of effort ever used even though such effort would be unreasonable under the circumstances. Preferred phrases: bona fide effort, reasonable effort or diligent effort as appropriate or set minimum performance standards.

Bona fide effort

See Best effort.

Cancel or cancellation
See Terminate.

Certified or registered mail
Terms primarily used only in U.S.A. Do not use in international licenses unless each country has this kind of mail

Commencement date
See Effective date.

Composed of
See Consisting of.

Comprising
Means a group of items which includes those named and others not named - open ended. Other words and phrases sometimes used for the same meaning: including, such as. Preferred phrase: including but not limited to. See Consisting of and Composed of which are sometimes erroneously used to mean comprising.

Confidential Information
See Secrecy agreement.

Confidential Information
Means information not generally known to the public. Supplier may not necessarily own information. Other words and phrases sometimes used and in some instances erroneously for same meaning: proprietary information, secret information, trade secret, know-how. Preferred phrase: confidential information.

Consisting of
Means only those items mentioned - closed ended. Other phrase sometimes used for the same meaning: composed of. Preferred phrase: use the word "only" in conjunction with the above. See Comprising which is sometimes erroneously used to mean consisting of.

Contract
See Agreement.

Convey
Used in connection with real property and assignments, not often used in licensing. See Grand and Assign.

Corporate address
See Place of business.

Covenant not to sue
See Nonexclusive license.

Cross license
Means when each party to an agreement grants a license to the other on the same subject matter. Term is used most often as a title and not as a technical licensing term in the body of the agreement.

Customer
Usually a purchaser of goods or services, term is generic in time - first purchaser such as distributor or last purchaser such as retail purchaser. Terms sometimes used for same meaning: end user, purchasor. Preferred phrase: final customer if end user is intended or intermediate customer or direct customer is appropriate.

Domicile
Means place of residence, used in connection with tax law, should not be used in licenses. Sometimes used to indicate place of incorporation. See Place of business.

Down payment

See Lump sum.

Due diligence

A term used by investment bankers. Means evaluating the situation or technology within a short period of time. Not used in licensing.

Effective date

Means the date of agreement comes into full force and effect. Date may be before or after date of signing of agreement by all parties. Words and phrases sometimes used and in some instances erroneously for same meaning: execution date, agreement date, commencement date, signing date. Preferred phrase: effective date. See Execution date.

Election

A requirement to make a choice. Word sometimes used for same meaning: option. Preferred word: election when appropriate. See Option.

Employment agreement

An agreement between employer and employee usually including provisions setting forth obligations of employee regarding confidential information, assignment of inventions, and obligations after termination of employment. Normally does not deal with monetary matters. Words and phrases sometimes used for same meaning: technical agreement, secrecy agreement, confidentiality agreement, assignment agreement. Preferred phrase: employment agreement. See Secrecy agreement.

End user

Means final customer or purchaser. Is an idiomatic English term and may be difficult to translate. Preferred phrase: final customer. See Customer.

Exclusive license

Means licensor grants the licensee the sole right to practice the invention or use trademark to the exclusion of licensor and others; may be limited to territory, field, product or time; normally exclusive licensee has right to license others. Phrases sometimes used, and in some instances erroneously, for same meaning: sole license, single license, assignment, limited license. Preferred phrase: exclusive license. See Sole license.

Execution date

Means the date all parties have signed the agreement. Sometimes means the date an executory obligation has been fulfilled. Words and phrases sometimes used, and in some instances erroneously, for same meaning: agreement date, signing date, effective date of agreement. Preferred phrase: agreement execution date. See Effective date.

Expiration date

See Term of agreement.

Field of use

Relates to the scope of license, such as a particular product for a particular use. Should define product and area of use.

First option

See First refusal.

First refusal, right of

Right of one party of an agreement to receive a right, commitment or a license from the same product, or same territory, etc. Words and phrases sometimes used for same meaning: license, sublicense, immunity from suit, holds harmless, covenant not to sue. Preferred phrase: nonexclusive license.

Option

Right to make a choice, not a requirement. Word sometimes used for same meaning: election. Preferred word: option. See Election.

Owned

See Proprietary rights.

Paid-up license

A license which does not require further royalties because some consideration has been given in advance including cash but not necessarily cash. Phrase sometimes used for same meaning: royalty free license. Preferred phrase: Paid up license with no future royalty payments.

Permission

See License.

Personal license

Idiomatic English, means a nonassignable, nontransferable license, usually license terminates on death of individual or dissolution or merger of corporation or firm.

Place of business

Means principal place of business or corporate offices. Words and phrases sometimes used for same meaning: domicile, corporate address, place of incorporation, location of corporate offices, principal place of business. Preferred phrase: a place of business. See Domicile.

Place of incorporation

Used primarily for identification purposes in license agreements. See Place of business and Domicile.

Principal place of business

See Place of business.

Promise or promissory

See Minimum royalty.

Proprietary information

Means information owned by supplier but not necessarily confidential. Misused to mean confidential information. Words and phrases sometimes used for same meaning: confidential information, all rights and title in intellectual property, owned, controlled. Preferred phrase: proprietary information. See Confidential information and Intellectual property.

Proprietary rights

Rights conferred by law for ownership or control (generic). Words and phrases sometimes used for same meaning: patent, trademark and copyright rights, license rights, intellectual property rights, right, proprietary information, title, confidential information. Preferred phrase: proprietary rights.

Public domain

Means free to use; free of patent, trademark and copyright rights. Misnomer for generally known to the public. Words and phrases sometimes used for same meaning: nonconfidential, not secret, publicly known, available to the public. In the context of nonconfidentiality, preferred phrase: generally known to the public or available to the public (something that is available to public may not be generally known to public).

The following is a list of categories for trade shows held in the U.S. and Canada. For information on a specific show, contact:
Trade Show Bureau
1660 Lincoln Street, Suite 2080
Denver, CO 80264-2001
Tel. (303) 860-7626
Fax (303) 860-7479

ACCOUNTING
- Auditors
- Financial Executives

ADVERTISING & PUBLIC RELATIONS
- Direct Mail
- Exhibits
- Incentive Marketing
- Mail Order
- Merchandising
- Premiums
- Promotion
- Public Relations
- Signs

AGRICULTURE
- Arborists
- Beekeepers
- Conservation
- Farmers
- Feed
- Fertilizers
- Grain
- Grange
- Herbs
- Growers
- Horticulture
- Irrigation
- Land Improvement
- Pest Control
- Plant Food
- Seeds
- Soil

AMUSEMENTS
- Dance
- Films
- Magicians
- Motion Pictures
- Recycling
- Theaters

APPAREL, FASHION & TEXTILE
- Fashion
- Handweavers
- Knitwear
- Retail Merchants
- Textiles
- Wool

ARMED SERVICES & VETERANS
- Veterans

ARTS

AUTOMOTIVE
- Bicycles
- Car Wash
- Cycles
- Engines
- Motorcycles
- Motors
- Parking
- Racing Cars
- Tires

AVIATION
- Air Freight

BANKING, CREDIT & FINANCE
- Brokers
- Collectors
- Consumers
- Credit
- Finance
- Investment
- Investors
- Mortgages
- Savings
- Securities

BARBER, BEAUTICIANS & COSMETICS
- Beauticians
- Cosmetics
- Hairdressers

BEVERAGE
- Beer
- Bottlers
- Bottles
- Brewers
- Coffee
- Liquor
- Soft Drinks
- Tea
- Wholesalers
- Wine

BUILDING & BUILDING MATERIALS
- Aggregates
- Apartments
- Architects
- Construction
- Contractors

Elevators
General Contractors
Roads
Roofing
Sand & Gravel
Slurry Seals
Surveying
BUSINESS & MANAGEMENT
Association Executives
Auctions
Auditoriums
Commerce
Consumers
Dealers
Direct Selling
Distributors
Executives
Franchise
Industrial Development
Industrial Relations
Inventions
Management
Manufacturers
Marketing
Meeting
Merchandise
Patents
Personnel
Producers
Purchasing
Retailers
Secretaries
Stores
Trade Fairs
Training
Vendors
Wholesalers
CEMETERIES & FUNERAL DIRECTORS
Funeral Directors
Monuments
Morticians
CERAMICS & GLASS
Glass
CHAMBERS OF COMMERCE
Convention Bureaus
Jaycees
CHEMISTRY
Laboratories
Renderers
Soap
CHIROPODY
Podiatry
CHIROPRACTIC

CLEANING, DYEING & LAUNDRY
Dry Cleaning
Fabricare
Laundry
CLUBS
COAL & PETROLEUM
Fuel
Gas
Geologists
Oil
COMMUNICATIONS
Fax
Telegraph
Telephones
COMPUTERS
Data Processing
CONTAINERS
Packaging
DAIRY
Cattle
Milk
DECORATING & DECORATING SUPPLIES
Floor Coverings
Interior Designers
Paint
Wallcoverings
DENTAL
EDUCATION
Alumni
Audio Visuals
Colleges
Consumers
Heating
History
Home Economics
Industrial Clubs
Museums
Parents
Personnel Guidance
Political Science
Schools
Sociology
Speech
Universities
Vocational
ELECTRICAL & ELECTRONICS
Acoustics
Broadcasters
Data Processing
Electronics
High Fidelity
Instrumentation
Radios

Zoos

HEATING, PLUMBING & REFRIGERATION
Air Conditioning
Ice
Plumbing
Refrigeration
Sheet Metal

HOBBIES & TOYS
Antiques
Bottles
Coins
Collectors
Craft
Do-it-yourself
Guns
Handicrafts
Numismatics
Philatelics
Post Cards
Railroads
Stamps
Toys
Watches

HOME SHOWS
Home & Gardens

HOSPITALS
Health Care
Nursing Homes

HOTELS & RESTAURANTS
Catering
Food Service
Hospitality
Restaurants

HOUSE FURNISHINGS
Appliances
Canvas
Floor Coverings
Furniture
Kitchens
Rugs

INSURANCE
Actuaries
Adjusters
Civic
Commercial Travelers
Property
Underwriters

LABOR UNIONS
Iron
Machinists
Magicians
Unions

LAW

Courts
Forensic Sciences
Judges
Parliamentarians
Patents
Trials

LEATHER & LEATHER PRODUCTS
Luggage
Shoes

LIBRARIES
Archivists
Books

LIVESTOCK
Animals
Cattle
Horses
Kennels
Pets
Range Management
Wildlife
Wool

MACHINERY
Engines
Fluid Power
Machine Tools
Materials Handling
Tools
Transmissions

MEDICAL
Anesthesiologists
Biofeedback
Colleges
Drugs
Nuclear
Obstetrics
Orthopedics
Podiatrist
Psychiatry
Radiology
Universities

METAL & METAL PRODUCTS
Foundrymen
Iron
Powder
Sheet Metal
Steel
Welding

MINERALS & MINING
Gems
Metallurgy

MISCELLANEOUS

MUSIC
Bands

COMPANIES LOOKING FOR INVENTIONS

The following is a partial list of companies that have a history of dealing with outside inventions. I suggest that you consult the Thomas Register or U.S. Industrial Directory for addresses, telephone and fax numbers and other information.

Kimberly-Clark Corporation
Koppers Company, Inc.
Arthur D. Little, Inc.
Merk & Company, Inc.
Monsanto
Nordson Corp.
Olin Corporations
Owens-Corning Fiberglas Corp.
Pfizer, Inc.
The Proctor & Gamble Company
The Quaker Oats Company
Raytheon Co.
Research Corp.
Reynolds Aluminum
A. H. Robins Company, Inc.
Rohm and Haas Company

Signode Corporation
Singer Company
SKF Industries, Inc.
SMC Corporation
Smith Kline Corporation
Sun Chemical Co.
Sunkist Growers, Inc.
Sybron Corp.
3M Company
TRW
Union Carbide Corp.
Uniroyal
Upjohn Company
Warner-Lambert
Westvaco Corporation
Xerox

Sample Of Letter You May Receive From Potential Licensee
(NOT FOR USE)

Dear,

We appreciate your desire to submit an idea to us for consideration. As you undoubtedly know, we retain many specialists both within and outside our organization to keep us constantly supplied with ideas. In addition, unsolicited submissions frequently come to us from others. In order to avoid misunderstanding and protect both the submitter and ourselves, we have adopted a uniform policy for consideration of all ideas submitted to us by persons outside our organization. Our policy is as follows:

We suggest that both your interest and ours would be best served if you consult a qualified attorney about possible legal means of protecting your idea before submitting it to us. You, of course, must be the sole judge of the type of protection you need or desire, including whether or not you consult a competent attorney.

If you desire to submit an idea to us without seeking such advice and protection, we strongly urge that you prepare a complete description of it in duplicate, have it dated and witnessed before a notary, retain one of the originals for yourself and forward the other to us.

We shall consider any idea you wish to submit to us provided this letter is signed by you indicating your understanding of, and agreement to, its contents. So that we may give your submission full consideration, it should be accompanied by all pertinent information in your possession regarding the matter.

We will advise you within a reasonable period of time after receipt of your idea whether or not we have any interest in it. If we have such interest, we will endeavor to reach a mutually satisfactory agreement with you.

It is possible that we may find that your idea is not new, or is in the public domain, or has already been investigated and considered by us. In such event, we would obviously have the right to proceed in such areas without any obligation to you. We do not ordinarily disclose our reasons for rejecting the idea you have submitted, although we will try to do so.

All submissions to us are voluntary, and receipt or retention by us shall be deemed for no other purpose than examination under the above conditions. If the foregoing is acceptable to you, please execute and return the duplicate original to us together with the details of your idea, and we shall be happy to consider your submissions.

Very truly yours,

ACKNOWLEDGED, ACCEPTED AND AGREED TO:

Dated:

SAMPLE PATENT AND PATENT DRAWING

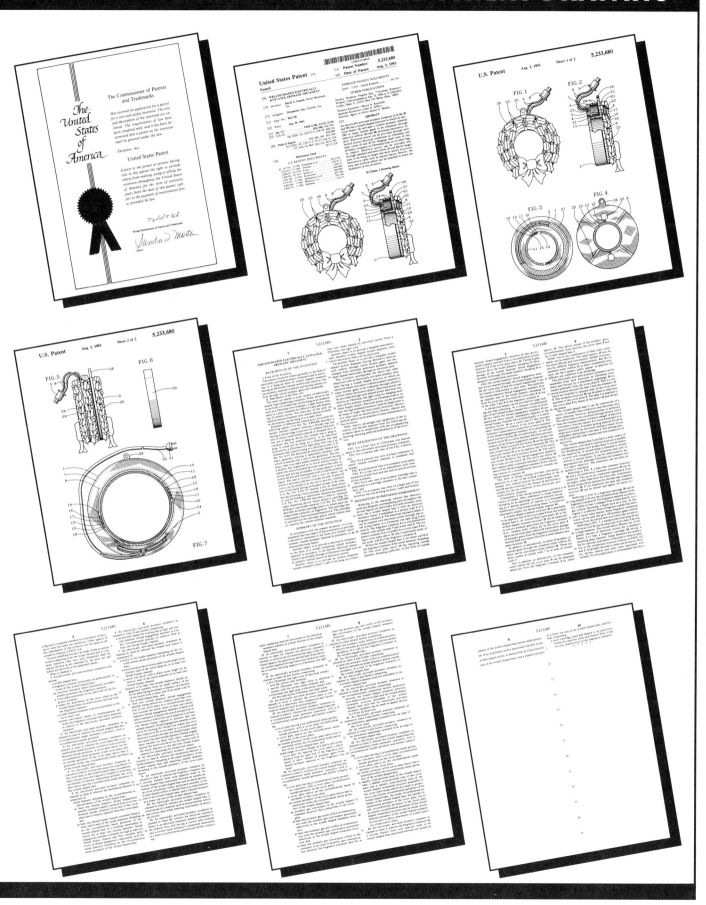

A workbook for inventors would not be complete without the necessary support and protection forms every aspiring or seasoned inventor needs. Through years of experience, I have compiled the following collection of forms. These will save you hundreds of dollars as you proceed through the development steps outlined in my tape series and this book.

Each form is uniquely designed with you in mind. Simply detach the perforated forms from the workbook and make as many photocopies as you need. I suggest you make a file folder for each form, which will give you a safe place to store the original and the copies for quick reference. Also, you may personalize these forms as you feel necessary.

CONFIDENTIALITY AGREEMENT

Agreement and acknowledgement
between_____(Inventor),
and_____ (Undersigned Company).

Whereas, the Inventor agrees to furnish the undersigned certain confidential information relating to the affairs of the Inventor for purposes of : (Describe)

,and

Whereas, the undersigned agrees to review, examine, inspect or obtain such information only for the purposes described above, and to otherwise hold such information confidential pursuant to the terms of this agreement,

BE IT KNOWN, that the Inventor has or shall furnish to the undersigned certain confidential information, as set forth on attached list, and may further allow the undersigned the right to inspect the development of the Inventor's new product concept including, but not limited to, the prototypes and interviewing employees or representatives of the Company, all on the following conditions:

1.   The undersigned agrees to hold all confidential or proprietary information or trade secrets("information") in trust and confidence and agrees that it shall be used only for the contemplated purpose, shall not be used for any other purpose or disclosed to any third party.

2.   No copies will be made or retained of any written information supplied.

3.   At the conclusion of the discussions, or upon demand by the Inventor, all information, including written notes, photographs, memoranda, technical drawings, or all notes taken by the undersigned shall be returned.

4.   This information shall not be disclosed to any employee or consultant unless those third parties agreed to execute and be bound by the terms of this agreement.

5.   It is understood that the undersigned shall have no obligation with respect to any information known by the undersigned or generally known within the industry prior to date of this agreement, or that which becomes common knowledge within the industry thereafter.

_____   _____
Date   Inventor

_____   _____
Date   Company

DISCLOSURE SUBJECT MATERIAL: _____
_____
_____
_____
_____
_____
_____
_____
_____
_____

CONSULTANT AGREEMENT

Parties: This agreement is made between the following parties:

Name(s)_____
Address_____
_____
(hereinafter called Inventor), and

Name(s):_____
Address:_____
_____
(hereinafter called Consultant).

Invention:_____
_____
_____

Duties Agreed to Perform: _____
_____
_____

Compensation Schedule:_____
_____
_____

Recitals: Inventor has one or more ideas relating to the above invention and desires to retain the services of the above consultant to perform the duties as specified. The Consultant has certain skills and knowledge desired by the Inventor relating to performance of the above duties.

Performance: Consultant will perform the above duties for the Inventor in accordance with the above duties and compensation schedule and the Inventor agrees to the above payment schedule.

Intellectual Property: All intellectual property, including possible trademarks, drawings, information, trade secrets, inventions, discoveries, or any improvements thereof, whether or not patentable, which are discovered, written or constructed that arise out of or related to the work performed by the above consultant in accordance with this agreement, are, or shall become the sole exclusive property of the Inventor.

Trade Secrets: Consultant recognizes that all information relating to the above invention disclosed to the Consultant by the Inventor, and all information generated by the Consultant during the performance of the above duties, become valuable trade secrets. Consultant shall treat all such information as confidential, during and after the performance of the above duties under this agreement. Consultant shall not reveal, publish, or communicate any of this information to anyone other than the Inventor, except upon the the express written authorization of the Inventor.

Return of Property: Consultant agrees to return all written materials and tangible property received from the Inventor, to return to the Inventor all property and copies of information supplied by the Inventor and all written materials resulting from or relating to work performed under this agreement, and not to deliver to any person, organization, or cause to be published, any such written material without prior written authorization.

Conflicts of Interest: Consultant recognizes a fiduciary obligation to Inventor arising out of the work and services performed in accordance with this agreement and accordingly will not offer Consultant services to or perform services for any competitor, potential or actual, of Inventor for the above project, or perform any other acts which may result in any conflict of interest by Consultant, during and after the term of this Agreement.

Mediation And Arbitration: If any dispute arises under this Agreement, both parties shall negotiate in good faith to settle such dispute. If the parties cannot resolve such disputes themselves, then either party may submit the dispute to deviation by a mediator approved by both parties. If the parties cannot reach an agreement with the mediator, or if either party does not wish to abide by the decision of the mediator, they shall submit the dispute to arbitration by any mutually acceptable arbitrator, or the American Arbitration Association. The costs of the arbitration proceeding shall be borne according to the decision of the arbitrator, who may apportion cost equally, or in accordance with any finding or fault or lack of good faith of either party. The arbitrator's award shall be non-appealable and enforceable in any court of competent jurisdiction.

Governing Law: This Agreement shall be governed by and interpreted under and according to the laws of the State of _____.

Signatures: The parties have indicated their agreement to all of the above terms and conditions by signing this Agreement on the respective dates as indicated below.

Date:_____   _____
                          Inventor

Date:_____   _____
                          Consultant

IN THE UNITED STATES PATENT AND TRADEMARK OFFICE

Honorable Commissioner of Patents and Trademarks,

Washington, D. C. 20231

Sir:

DISCLOSURE DOCUMENT

The undersigned, being the inventor of the disclosed invention, requests that the enclosed papers be accepted under the Disclosure Document Program, and that they be preserved for a period of two years.

Duplicate copies of this letter and the disclosure, together with a check in the amount of US$10.00, and a stamped, self-addressed envelope, are filed herewith.

Respectfully submitted,

_____

inventor

_____

_____

address

FACSIMILE TRANSMISSION

Date: Number of pages:

To: Fax No:

From: Fax No:

Re:

Message:_____

_____
_____
_____
_____
_____
_____
_____
_____
_____
_____
_____
_____
_____
_____
_____
_____

The Secret To Making Your Invention A Reality

INVENTION DIARY

Date of Conception :

Description and Operation:

_____

_____

_____

_____

_____

_____

_____

_____

_____

_____

_____

_____

_____

Inventor's Name: _____ Date: _____

Witnessed: _____ Date: _____

Witnessed: _____ Date: _____

INVENTION RECORD

Page _____ of _____

On the space provided below, describe your invention and make a drawing as you see it in your mind. Briefly describe the materials to be used and the method of manufacturing. Sign and date this record and have two witnesses sign and date the record as evidence that you are the inventor of this concept. This is your record of the date of conception, and may be valuable if your patent application is disputed by another inventor claiming that he or she conceived that idea first. THIS DOES NOT TAKE THE PLACE OF A PATENT APPLICATION.

Inventor's Name: _____ Date: _____

Witnessed: _____ Date: _____

Witnessed: _____ Date: _____

Inventors'
DIGEST

AMERICA'S ONLY INVENTORS' MAGAZINE

Everything you always wanted to know about inventing!

Since 1985, INVENTORS' DIGEST has been giving inventors the information they *need* to bring their products to market.

Do you need a patent search?
Do you need an objective evaluation?
Do you need legal services?
Do you need marketing help?
Do you need to find out if a company is honest?
Do you need to sell or license the rights to your invention?
Do you need to network with successful inventors?

If you answered "Yes" to any of these questions,
THEN YOU <u>NEED</u> INVENTORS' DIGEST!!!

Don't just take our word for it . . . read what other inventors say:

"INVENTORS' DIGEST is the single most informative publication on the invention process that I have yet encountered. I learn something valuable in every issue. (And I bought all the back issues, too.)" David C. Woodruff, Berne, Indiana

"I was President of the Inventors Institute of Alaska for three years. I highly recommend your magazine to all the inventors. With your help, many questions were answered that helped me go from idea to market much faster. I now have protection, manufacturing capabilities, and a market. And, best of all, created new jobs! Keep up the good work!" James D. James, Wasilla, Alaska

"I like it! I like it! I got my money's worth on the first issue. Why did I wait so long?" Leon T. Swilley, Dover, Florida

Don't *you* wait!!! Call today!!!
1-800-838-8808

The Secret To Making Your Invention A Reality

INVENTOR'S QUESTIONNAIRE

The company that you are making a submission to may have questions that will help them better evaluate your new product idea or invention. The following questionnaire includes some most frequently asked. This is your opportunity to put down all your thoughts concerning your invention and why you feel your product will be successful.

1) How did you come up with the idea for this invention?_____
_____

2) What brought you to the understanding that your invention was marketable?
_____

3) How long have you been working on this invention?_____

4) Have you filed for a United States patent?_____

5) Have you submitted your invention to other companies? _____If yes, list the names:
_____

6) In sharing your invention concept with others, what reactions has it received?
_____

7) If you were a salesman and were selling this new product, what list of benefits would you tell your prospective buyers?_____
_____

8) What distinguishable features make this product unique?_____
_____

9) Have you seen any similar products available in stores or catalogs? Name the manufacture(s), model number(s), and price(s):_____
_____

10) What would your suggested retail price be for this new item and what is your reason?
_____

Continued on back.

11) Do you have an approximate manufacturing cost?_____

12) What would you sell this item to retailers for?_____

13) What accounts would you sell to?_____
_____

14) What advantages does your invention have over similar products existing out in the marketplace?_____
_____

15) Have you applied for a Trademark? _____If no, what names are you considering for your invention? _____

16) Who are the primary users of this product?_____
_____

17) Who are the secondary users of this product?_____
_____

18) Use this space below and any additional space necessary to provide any other information that you feel is important as we consider whether your invention fits within our company product line.

_____   _____
Date Submitted   Signature

_____   _____
Print or Type Name   Address

LICENSE AGREEMENT

AGREEMENT made this _____ day of _____ 19___, between

_____ (hereinafter called "Licensor"), and

_____ (hereinafter called "Licensee"):

WITNESSETH:

WHEREAS Licensor has rights to the name, character, symbol, design, likeness and visual representation of_____ (which name, character, symbol, design, likeness and visual representation and/or each of the individual components thereof shall hereinafter be called the "Name"), said Name having been used over the facilities of numerous stations in radio and/or television broadcasting and in allied fields, and in promotional and advertising material in different businesses and being well known and recognized by the general public and associated in the public mind with Licensor, and

WHEREAS Licensee desires to utilize the Name upon and in connection with the manufacture, sale and distribution of articles hereinafter described,

NOW, THEREFORE, in consideration of the mutual promises herein contained, it is hereby agreed:

1. GRANT OF LICENSE.
   (a) Articles. Upon the terms and conditions hereinafter set forth, Licensor hereby grants to Licensee and Licensee hereby accepts the right, license and privilege of utilizing the Name solely and only upon and in connection with the manufacture, sale and distribution of the following articles:

   (b) Territory. The license hereby granted extends only to _____.

Licensee agrees that it will not make or authorize, any use, direct or indirect, of the Name in any other area, and that it will not knowingly sell articles covered by this agreement to persons who intend or are likely to resell them in any other area.

   (c) Term. The term of the license hereby granted shall be effective on the ____ day of _____ 19_____, and shall continue until the _____ day of _____ 19___, unless sooner terminated in accordance with the provisions hereof.

2. TERMS OF PAYMENT.
   (a) Rate. Licensee agrees to pay Licensor as royalty a sum equal to _____ percent (____%) of all net sales by Licensee or any of its affiliated, associated or subsidiary companies of the articles covered by this agreement. The term "net sales" shall mean gross sales less quantity discounts and returns, but no deduction shall be made for cash or other discounts or uncollectible accounts. No costs incurred in the manufacture, sale, distribution or exploitation of the articles shall be deducted from any royalty payable by Licensee.

(b) Minimum Royalties. Licensee agrees to pay to Licensor a minimum royalty of _____ dollars ($_____) as a minimum guarantee against royalties to be paid to Licensor during the first contract year, said minimum royalty to be paid on or before _____. The advance sum of _____ dollars($_____)paid on the signing hereof shall be applied against such guarantee. No part of such minimum royalty shall in any event be repayable to Licensee.

(c) Periodic Statements. Within thirty (30) days after the initial shipment of the articles covered by this agreement, and promptly on the 15th of each calendar month thereafter, Licensee shall furnish to Licensor complete and accurate statements certified to be accurate by Licensee showing the number, description, and gross sale price, itemized deductions from gross sales price and net sales price of the articles covered by this agreement distributed and/or sold by Licensee during the preceding calendar month, together with any returns made during the preceding calendar month. For this purpose, Licensee shall use the statement form attached hereto, copies of which form may be obtained by Licensee from Licensor. Such statements shall be furnished to Licensor whether or not any of the articles have been sold during the preceding calendar month.

(d) Royalty Payments. Royalties in excess of the aforementioned minimum royalty shall be due on the 15th day of the month following the calendar month in which earned, and payment shall accompany the statements furnished as required above.   The receipt or acceptance by Licensor of any of the statements furnished pursuant to this agreement or of any royalties paid hereunder (or the cashing of any royalty checks paid hereunder) shall not preclude Licensor from questioning the correctness thereof at any time, and in the event that any inconsistencies or mistakes are discovered in such statements or payments, they shall immediately be rectified and the appropriate payment made by Licensee.

3. EXCLUSIVITY.
(a) Nothing in this agreement shall be construed to prevent Licensor from granting any other licenses for the use of the Name or from utilizing the Name in any manner whatsoever, except that Licensor agrees that except as provided herein it will grant no other licenses for the territory to which this license extends effective during the term of this agreement, for the use of the Name in connection with the sale of the articles described in paragraph 1.

(b) It is agreed that if Licensor should convey an offer to Licensee to purchase any of the articles listed in paragraph 1, in connection with a premium, giveaway or other promotional arrangement, Licensee shall have ten (10) days within which to accept or reject such an offer. In the event that Licensee fails to accept such offer within the specified ten (10) days, Licensor shall have the right to enter into the proposed premium, giveaway or promotional arrangement using the services of another manufacturer, provided, however, that in such event Licensee shall have a three (3) day period within which to meet the best offer of such manufacturer for the production of such articles if the price of such manufacturer is higher than the price offered to Licensee by Licensor.

4. GOOD WILL, ETC.
Licensee recognizes the great value of the good will associated with the Name, and acknowledges that the Name and all rights therein and good will pertaining thereto belong exclusively to Licensor, and that the Name has a secondary meaning in the mind of the public.

5. LICENSOR'S TITLE AND PROTECTION OF LICENSOR'S RIGHTS
(a) Licensee agrees that it will not, during the term of this agreement, or thereafter, attack the title or any rights of Licensor in and to the Name or attack the validity of this license. Licensor hereby indemnifies Licensee and undertakes to hold it harmless against any claims or suits arising solely out of the use by Licensee of the Name as authorized in this agreement, provided that prompt notice is given to Licensor of any such claim or suit and provided, further, that Licensor shall have the option to undertake and conduct the defense of any suit so brought and no settlement of any such claim or suit is made without the prior written consent of Licensor.

(b) Licensee agrees to assist Licensor to the extent necessary in the procurement of any protection or to protect any of Licensor's rights to the Name, and Licensor, if it so desires may commence or prosecute any claims or suits in its own name or in the name of Licensee or join Licensee as a party thereto. Licensee shall notify Licensor in writing of any infringements or imitations by others of the Name on the articles similar to those covered by this agreement which may come to Licensee's attention, and Licensor shall have the sole right to determine whether or not any action shall be taken on account of any such infringements or imitations. Licensee shall not institute any suit or take any action on account of any such infringements or imitations without first obtaining the written consent of the Licensor so to do.

6. INDEMNIFICATION BY LICENSEE AND PRODUCT LIABILITY INSURANCE.

Licensee hereby indemnifies Licensor and undertakes to defend Licensee and/or Licensor against and hold Licensor harmless from any claims, suits, loss and damage arising out of any allegedly unauthorized use of any patent, process, idea, method or device by Licensee in connection with the articles covered by this agreement or any other alleged action by Licensee and also from any claims, suits, loss and damage arising out of alleged defects in the articles. Licensee agrees that is will obtain, at its own expense, product liability insurance from a recognized insurance company which has qualified to do business

in the State of _____, providing adequate protections (at least in the amount of $100,000/$300,000) for Licensor (as well as for Licensee) against any claims, suits, loss or damage arising out of any alleged defects in the articles. As proof of such insurance, a fully paid certificate of insurance naming Licensor as an insured party will be submitted to Licensor by Licensee for Licensor's prior approval before any article is distributed or sold, and at the latest within thirty (30) days after the date first written above; any proposed change in certificates of insurance shall be submitted to Licensor for its prior approval. Licensor shall be entitled to a copy of the then prevailing certificate of insurance, which shall be furnished Licensor by Licensee. A used in the first two sentences of this paragraph 6, "Licensor" shall also include the officers, directors, agents, and employees of the Licensor, or any of its subsidiaries or affiliates, any person(s) the use of whose name may be licensed hereunder, the package producer and the cast of the radio and/or television program whose name may be licensed hereunder, the stations over which the programs are transmitted, any sponsor of said programs and its advertising agency, and their respective officers, directors, agents and employees.

7. QUALITY OF MERCHANDISE

Licensee agrees that the articles covered by this agreement shall be of high standard and of such style, appearance and quality as to be adequate and suited to their exploitation to the best advantage and to the protection and enhancement of the Name and the good will pertaining thereto, that such articles will be manufactured, sold and distributed in accordance with all applicable Federal, State and local laws, and that the policy of sale, distribution, and/or exploitation by Licensee shall be of high standard and to the best advantage and that the same shall in no manner reflect adversely upon the good name of the Licensor or any of its programs or the Name. To this end Licensee shall, before selling or distributing any of the articles, furnish to Licensor free of cost, for its written approval, a reasonable number of samples of each article, its cartons, containers and packaging or wrapping material. The quality and style of such articles as well as of any carton, container or packing or wrapping material shall be subject to approval of Licensor. Any item submitted to Licensor shall not be deemed approved unless and until the same shall be approved b Licensor in writing. After samples have been approved pursuant to this paragraph, Licensee shall not depart therefrom in any material respect without Licensor's prior written consent, and Licensor shall not withdraw its approval of the approved sample except on sixty (60) days prior written notice to Licensee. From time to time after Licensee has commenced selling the articles and upon Licensor's written request, Licensee shall furnish without cost to Licensor not more than ten (10) additional random samples of each article being manufactured and sold by Licensee hereunder, together with any cartons, containers and packing and wrapping material used in connection therewith.

8. LABELING

(a) Licensee agrees that it will cause to appear on or within each article sold by it under this license and on or within all advertising, promotional or display material bearing the Name the notice "Copyright © (year) _____" and any other notice

desired by Licensor and, where such article or advertising, promotional or display material bears a trademark or service mark, appropriate statutory notice of registration or application for registration thereof. In the event that any article is marketed in a carton, container and/or packing or wrapping material bearing the Name, such notice shall also appear upon the said carton, container and/or packing or wrapping material. Each and every tag, label, imprint or other device containing any such notice and all advertising, promotional or display material bearing the Name shall be submitted by Licensee to Licensor for its written approval prior to use by Licensee. Approval by Licensor shall not constitute waiver of Licensor's rights or Licensee's duties under any provision of this agreement.

(b) Licensee agrees to cooperate fully and in good faith with Licensor for the purpose of securing and preserving Licensor's (or any grantor of Licensor's) rights in and to the Name. In the event there has been no previous registration of the Name and/or articles and/or any material relating thereto, Licensee shall, at Licensor's request and expense, register such as a copyright, trademark and/or service mark in the appropriate class in the name of Licensor or, if Licensor so requests, in Licensee's own name. However, it is agreed that nothing contained in this agreement shall be construed as an assignment or grant to the Licensee of any right, title or interest in or to the Name, it being understood that all rights relating thereto are reserved by Licensor, except for the license hereunder to Licensee of the right to use and utilize the Name only as specifically and expressly provided in this agreement. Licensee hereby agrees that at the termination or expiration of this agreement Licensee will be deemed to have assigned, transferred and conveyed to Licensor any trade rights, equities, good will, titles or other rights in and to the Name which may have been obtained by Licensee or which may have been vested in Licensee in pursuance of any endeavors covered hereby, and that Licensee will execute any instruments requested by Licensor to accomplish or confirm the foregoing. Any such assignment, transfer or conveyance shall be without other consideration than the mutual covenants and considerations of this agreement.

(c) Licensee hereby agrees that its every use of such Name shall inure to the benefit of Licensor and that Licensee shall not at any time acquire any rights in such Name by virtue of any use it may make of such Name.

9. PROMOTIONAL MATERIAL

(a) In all cases where Licensee desires artwork involving articles which are the subject of this license to be executed, the cost of such artwork and the time for the production thereof shall be borne by Licensee. All artwork and designs involving the Name, or any reproduction thereof shall, notwithstanding their invention or use by Licensee, be and remain the property of Licensor and Licensor shall be entitled to use the same and to license the use of the same by others.

(b) Licensor shall have the right, but shall not be under any obligation, to use the Name and/or the name of Licensee so as to give the Name, Licensee, Licensor and/or Licensor's programs full and favorable prominence and publicity. Licensor shall not be under any obligation whatsoever to continue broadcasting any radio or television program or use the Name of any person, character, symbol, design or likeness or visual representation thereof in any radio or television program.

(c)Licensee agrees not to offer for sale or advertise or publicize any of the articles licensed hereunder on radio or television without the prior written approval of Licensor, which approval Licensor may grant or withhold in its unfettered discretion.

10. DISTRIBUTION

(a) Licensee agrees that during the term of this license it will diligently and continuously manufacture, distribute and sell the articles covered by this agreement and that it will make and maintain adequate arrangement for the distribution of the articles.

(b) Licensee agrees that it will sell and distribute the articles covered by this agreement outright at a competitive price and at not more than the price generally and customarily charged the trade by the Licensee and not on an approval, consignment or sale or return basis, and only to jobbers, wholesalers and distributors for sale and distribution to retail stores and merchants, and to retail stores and merchants for sale and distribution direct to the public. Licensee shall not, without prior written consent of Licensor, sell or distribute such articles to jobber, wholesalers, distributors, retail stores or merchants whose sales or distribution are or will be made for publicity or promotional tie-in purposes, combination sales, premiums, giveaways, or similar methods of merchandising, or whose business methods are questionable. In the event any sale is made at a special price to any of Licensee's subsidiaries or to any other person, firm or corporation related in any matter to Licensee or its officers, directors or major stockholders, there shall be a royalty paid on such sales based upon the price generally charged the trade by Licensee.

(c) Licensee agrees to sell to Licensor such quantities of the articles at as low a rate and on as good terms as Licensee sells similar quantities of the articles to the general trade.

11. RECORDS

Licensee agrees to keep accurate books of account and records covering all transactions relating to the license hereby granted, and Licensor and its duly authorized representatives shall have the right at all reasonable hours of the day to an examination of said books of account and records and of all other documents and materials in the possession or under the control of Licensee with respect to the subject matter and terms of this agreement, and shall have free and full access thereto for said purposes and for the purpose of making extracts therefrom. Upon demand of Licensor, Licensee shall at its own expense furnish to Licensor a detailed statement by an independent certified public accountant showing the number, description, gross sales price, itemized deductions from the gross sales price and net sales price of the articles covered by this agreement distributed and/or sold by Licensee to the date of Licensor's demand. All books of account and records shall be kept available for at least two (2) years after the termination of this license.

12. BANKRUPTCY, VIOLATION, ETC.

(a) If Licensee shall not have commenced in good faith to manufacture and distribute in substantial quantities all the articles listed in paragraph 1 within three (3) months after the date of this agreement of is at any time thereafter in any calendar month Licensee fails to sell any of the articles (or any class or category of the articles), Licensor in addition to all other remedies available to it hereunder may terminate this license with respect to any articles or class or category thereof which have not been manufactured and distributed during such month, by giving written notice of termination to Licensee. Such notice shall be effective when mailed to Licensee.

(b) If Licensee files a petition in bankruptcy or is adjudicated a bankrupt or if a petition in bankruptcy is filed against Licensee or if it becomes insolvent, or makes an assignment for the benefits of its creditors or an arrangement pursuant to any bankruptcy law, or if Licensee discontinues its business or if a receiver is appointed for it or its business, the license hereby granted shall automatically terminate forthwith with out any notice whatsoever being necessary. in the event this license is so terminated, Licensee, its receivers, representatives, trustees, agents, administrators, successors and/or assigns shall have no right to sell, exploit or in any way deal with or in any articles covered by this agreement or any carton, container, packing or wrapping material, advertising, promotional or display material pertaining thereto, except with and under the special consent and instructions of Licensor in writing, which they shall be obligated to follow.

(c) If Licensee shall violate any of its other obligations under the terms of this agreement, Licensor shall have the right to terminate the license hereby granted upon ten (10) days' notice in writing, and such notice of termination shall become effective unless Licensee shall completely remedy the violation within the ten-day period and satisfy Licensor that such violation has been remedied.

(d) Termination of the license under the provisions of paragraph 12 shall be without prejudice to any rights which Licensor may otherwise have against Licensee. Upon the termination of this license, notwithstanding anything to the contrary herein, all royalties on sales theretofore made shall become immediately due and payable and no minimum royalties shall be repayable.

13. SPONSORSHIP BY COMPETITIVE PRODUCT.

In the event that any of the articles listed in paragraph 1 conflicts with any product of a present or future sponsor of a program on which the Name appears or is used, or with any product of a subsidiary of affiliate of such sponsor, then Licensor shall have the right to terminate this agreement as to such article or articles by written notice to Licensee effective not less than thirty (30) days after the date such notice is given. In the event of such termination, Licensee shall have sixty (60) days after the effective date of such termination to dispose of all of such articles on hand or in process of manufacture prior to such notice, in accordance with the provisions of paragraph 15. However, in the event such termination is effective as to all the articles subject to this agreement and the advance guarantee for the then current year has not been fully accounted for by actual royalties by the end of the sixty (60) day disposal period, Licensor shall refund to Licensee the difference between the advance guarantee which has been paid for such contract year and the actual royalties. The refund provision contained in the preceding sentence pertains only to termination occurring pursuant to this paragraph 13, and shall not affect the applicability of any other paragraph to such termination except as expressly contradicted herein.

14. FINAL STATEMENT UPON TERMINATION OF EXPIRATION

Sixty (60) days before the expiration of this license and, in the event of its termination, ten (10) days after receipt of notice of termination or the happening of the event which terminates this agreement where no notice is required, a statement showing the number and description of articles covered by this agreement on hand or in process shall be furnished by Licensee to Licensor. Licensor shall have the right to take a physical inventory to ascertain or verify such inventory and statement, and refusal by Licensee to submit to such physical inventory by Licensor shall forfeit Licensee's right to dispose of such inventory, Licensor retaining all other legal and equitable rights Licensor may have in the circumstances.

15. DISPOSAL OF STOCK UPON TERMINATION OR EXPIRATION.

After termination of the license under the provisions of paragraph 12, Licensee, except as otherwise provided in the agreement, may dispose of articles covered by this agreement which are on hand or in process at the time notice of termination is received for a period of sixty (60) days after notice of termination, provided advances and royalties with respect to that period are paid and statements are furnished for that period in accordance with paragraph 2. Notwithstanding anything to the contrary herein, Licensee shall not manufacture, sell or dispose of any articles covered by this license after its expiration or its termination based on the failure of Licensee to affix notice of copyright, trademark or service mark registration or any other notice to the articles, cartons, containers, or packing or wrapping material or advertising, promotional or display material, or because of the departure by Licensee from the quality and style approved by Licensor pursuant to paragraph 7.

16. EFFECT OF TERMINATION OF EXPIRATION

Upon and after the expiration or termination of this license, all rights granted to Licensee hereunder shall forthwith revert to Licensor, who shall be free to license others to use the Name in connection with the manufacture, sale and distribution of the articles covered hereby and Licensee will refrain from further use of the Name or any further reference to it, direct or indirect, or anything deemed by Licensor to be similar to the Name in connection with the manufacture, sale or distribution of Licensee's products, except as provided in paragraph 15.

17. LICENSOR'S REMEDIES

(a) Licensee acknowledges that its failure (except as otherwise provided herein) to commence in good faith to manufacture and distribute in substantial quantities any one or more of the articles listed in paragraph 1 within three (3) months after the date of this agreement and to continue during the term hereof to diligently and continuously manufacture, distribute and sell the articles covered by this agreement or any class or category thereof will result in immediate damages to Licensor.

(b) Licensee acknowledges that its failure (except otherwise provided herein) to cease the manufacture, sale or distribution of the articles covered by this agreement or any class or category thereof at the termination or expiration of this agreement will result in immediate and irremediable damage to Licensor and to the rights of any subsequent license. Licensee acknowledges and admits that there is no adequate remedy at law for such failure to cease manufacture, sale or distribution, and Licensee agrees that in the event of such failure Licensor shall be entitled to equitable relief by way of temporary and permanent injunctions and such other further relief as any court with jurisdiction may deem just and proper.

(c) Resort to any remedies referred to herein shall not be construed as a waiver of any other rights and remedies to which Licensor in entitled under this agreement or otherwise.

18. EXCUSE FOR NONPERFORMANCE.

Licensee shall be released form its obligation hereunder and this license shall terminate in the event that governmental regulations or other causes arising out of a state of national emergency or war or causes beyond the control of the parties render performance impossible and one party so informs the other in writing of such causes and its desire to be so released. In such events, all royalties on sales theretofore made shall become immediately due and payable and no minimum royalties shall be repayable.

19. NOTICES

All notices and statements to be given, and all payments to be made hereunder, shall be given or made at the respective addresses of the parties as set forth above unless notification of a change of address is given in writing, and the date of mailing shall be deemed the date the notice or statement is given.

20. NO JOINT VENTURE

Nothing herein contained shall be construed to place the parties in the relationship of partners or joint venturers, and Licensee shall have no power to obligate or bind Licensor in any manner whatsoever.

21. NO ASSIGNMENT OR SUBLICENSE BY LICENSEE

This assignment and all rights and duties hereunder are personal to Licensee and shall not, without the written consent of Licensor, be assigned, mortgaged, sublicense or otherwise encumbered by Licensee or by operation of law. Licensor may assign but shall furnish written notice of assignment.

22. NO WAIVER, ETC.

None of the terms of this agreement can be waived or modified except by an express agreement in writing signed by both parties. There are no representations, promises, warranties, covenants or undertakings other than those contained in this agreement, which represents the entire understanding of the parties. The failure of either party hereto to enforce, or the delay by either party in enforcing, any of its rights under this agreement shall not be deemed a continuing waiver or a modification thereof and either party may, within the time provided by applicable law, commence appropriate legal proceeding to enforce any or all of such rights. No person, firm, group or corporation (whether included in the Name or otherwise) other than Licensee and Licensor shall be deemed to have acquired any rights by reason of anything contained in this agreement, except as provided in paragraphs 6 and 21.

This agreement shall be construed in accordance with the internal laws of the State_____.

IN WITNESS WHEREOF, the parties hereto have caused this instrument to be duly executed as of the day and year first above written.

_____
("Licensor")

By_____

Title:

_____
("Licensee")

By_____

Title:

LICENSE OPTION AGREEMENT

DATE:
INVENTOR:

POTENTIAL LICENSEE:

The following shall constitute an agreement between us relative to an option to license certain rights of my invention known as _____ patent number _____.

1. For the sum of $_____ paid to me herewith, I agree to grant you the irrevocable right and option for _____ (__) months from the date hereof to manufacture and sell the above products according to the terms of a mutually agreed upon "License Agreement".

2. I hereby warrant that I have the right to grant licenses under the United States letter patent, foreign patent and patent applications listed above.

3. I further hereby warrant and represent that during the time this Option is in effect, I shall not assign or encumber the patent rights in any way, nor make any commitment with respect thereto inconsistent with the terms of the Option.

4. Concurrently herewith we both have affixed our signatures to this Option Agreement. Not withstanding such signatures, the aforesaid agreement shall not become binding and effective except as provided in paragraphs 5 and 7 hereof.

5. This Option may be exercised by us at any time during the   month Option period by written notice sent by registered mail, return receipt requested, on or before the expiration date, addressed to you or me and sent to the respective address herein set forth.

6. (a) If we fail to exercise this Option as aforesaid, all of our rights hereafter shall cease in thirty days after the above date, and this agreement shall become null and void. (b) Within our sole discretion, however, we may decide to forego our Option hereunder at a date during the Option period. In such event, the company shall notify me in writing upon which event the terms of this paragraph 6, (a) shall immediately apply.

7. If we exercise this Option as aforesaid, the rights and obligations specified in the agreement shall become immediately effective.

The Secret To Making Your Invention A Reality

8. This agreement shall insure to the benefit of and shall be binding upon all successors and assigns and our successors and assigns.

If the above meets with your approval, kindly indicate your acceptance of the terms and conditions hereof by signing where indicated below and returning the signed copy of this Option Agreement to me.

Inventor

By: _____

Accepted and Agreed

Company:

By:_____

Title:_____

LICENSEE INFORMATION FORM

Researching the company's profile is important. Identify a minimum of 10 companies that might prove to be good prospects. Rank these companies in order of importance.

_____ Choice

Name: _____

Address: _____

Tel: _____ Fax: _____

Important Contact:_____

Is Company Public or Private?_____

Present Product Categories: _____

_____

_____

Annual Sales: _____

Advertising Budget: _____

Manufacturing Locations: _____

_____

_____

Recognized Company Brand Names: _____

Does Company Have History of Working with Inventors?_____

Major Competition: _____

_____

_____

Additional Information: _____

_____

_____

MARKET RESEARCH SURVEY

Name: _____

Address: _____

_____

Comments About the Product: _____

_____

_____

_____

_____

_____

Signature of Participant:_____Date:_____

Name: _____

Address: _____

_____

Comments About the Product:_____

_____

_____

_____

_____

_____

Signature of Participant:_____Date:_____

ORDER FORM

Call 1-800-334-0233 or fill out the order form below and send to:

Ventur-Training, Ltd.
3794 Meeting Street
Duluth, Ga. 30136

The Secret To Making Your Invention A Reality, (Tape Series) $49.95

The Secret To Making Your Invention A Reality, (The Book) $24.95

Georgia residents add 5% sales tax . . . . ._____

Shipping/Handling (for one or both) . . . .$ 5.50

TOTAL ENCLOSED . . . .$_____

_____
Name

_____
Address

_____
City, State, Zip

_____Check, _____Money Order or..........

_____
MasterCard/Visa Number (Circle one and write card number above)

_____   (_____)_____
Expiration Date   Home Phone Number

_____
Authorized Signature

ORDER FORM
PATENT AND TRADEMARK BOOKLETS

Date:

U.S. Government Printing Office
Superintendent of Documents
Mail Stop: SSOP
Washington, DC 20402-9328

Subject:
General Information Concerning Patents ISBN 0-16-037933-4 $2.25
Basic Facts About Trademarks ISBN 0-16-036162-1 $2.50

Please ship the above publications, I have enclosed a check for $ _____

Ship to the following address.

Name: _____

Address   _____

            _____

PATENT SEARCH WORKSHEET

Patent Number:_____Inventor_____

Description:_____

Major Claims:_____

_____

_____

Similarities to My Invention:_____

_____

_____

Patent Number:_____Inventor_____

Description:_____

Major Claims:_____

_____

_____

Similarities to My Invention:_____

_____

_____

Patent Number:_____Inventor_____

Description:_____

Major Claims:_____

_____

_____

Similarities to My Invention:_____

_____

_____

RECORD OF IMPORTANT CONTACTS

Name & Title   Date of Meeting   Confidential Agreement

_____   _____   _____

Address, Phone & Fax_____

_____

Comments:_____

_____

_____

Name & Title   Date of Meeting   Confidential Agreement

_____   _____   _____

Address, Phone & Fax_____

_____

Comments:_____

_____

_____

Name & Title   Date of Meeting   Confidential Agreement

_____   _____   _____

Address, Phone & Fax_____

_____

Comments:_____

_____

_____

SAMPLE SUBMISSION LETTER

Date:

The Name and Address of Company you are submitting to:

Attention: New Product Development Department

I am an entrepreneur/inventor and have developed a new product that would be well suited for your company. I have filed for a U.S. patent (or have received a patent). Would you please send me the necessary forms and policy guidelines for submitting an outside invention? I am interested in a potential licensing arrangement with your company.

In the event that your company does not provide a submission agreement, I have taken the liberty of enclosing a standard agreement used within most industries.

Thank you for your consideration. I look forward to your reply at your earliest convenience.

Sincerely,

Your Name, Address and Telephone Number
Your Title
Enclosures

TRADEMARK DESIGN RECORD

Name Selected _____

Trademark Design Recorded Below

Inventor's Name: _____ Date: _____

Witnessed: _____ Date: _____

Witnessed: _____ Date: _____

The Secret To Making Your Invention A Reality